AF228227

The TAO of FUNDRAISING

The TAO of FUNDRAISING

The Science, Philosophy, and Psychology behind Attracting Capital

BY JOHN KIM

With Seth Libby

Forefront
BOOKS

To Jodi, thank you for putting up with my fundraising obsession for so long. I'm proud to be the second most persuasive person in our family after you.
—John

To Liza, Lucas, and Mila. Every word is for you.
—Seth

CONTENTS

A NOTE ON THE TITLE

Dear Reader,

You have surely noticed that the title of this book is the "Tao" of Fundraising. My good friend, Josh Waitzkin, read the book and, while praising its contents in general, raised one particular objection about that title.

"Kimmer," he told me, "you may admire Taoism and even feel a certain inspiration from its ideas, but this isn't a book on Taoism. And you're no Taoist."

To be honest, he also took issue with the term "fundraising," feeling the book is about far more than that—but we'll get to that objection in a moment.

On the use of "Tao," he's absolutely right. This is not a book on Taoism nor is it based on traditional Taoist lessons and philosophies. I want to acknowledge up front that some may object to my use of such an ancient, venerable, and wise tradition when the book isn't framed around that philosophy.

So why have I chosen not to change the title?

On a certain, practical level, it is a simple marketing decision. Marketing is intimately related to fundraising, and I know a good marketing concept when I see it. Using a term like "Tao" is stickier than more conventional English words like "way" or "path." The term catches the curious eye and lodges in the mind. I was not willing to give up that advantage.

But this is not the only—or even main—reason I have left the title as it was originally conceived. When my co-author, Seth, and I discovered the title together in the course of the work of co-creation before you, we knew immediately it was the right choice because it so perfectly matched our deepest aspirations for the book.

Words and labels are powerful because they invoke emotions and beliefs. The word "Tao" suggests certain spiritual concepts and connections to life philosophy. And this is the deeper message of the pages you are about to read.

The subject of this book is fundraising, and I have done my best to provide practical advice on how to pursue that activity either for an individual project or as a profession.

However, as Josh suggested, fundraising is more our point of departure than our sole theme. In my experience, most books on sales focus on building relationships. This book shares that focus, but its scope is broader and deeper than that. On its most profound level, it is really about understanding the way we relate to the world around us. Yes, it is about the way we relate to other people. But it's also about the way we relate to money. To power. To emotions. To themselves.

It's about the way we relate to life.

Please keep this holistic concept in mind as you read this book. The ideas I present will make you a better fundraiser.

And, hopefully, the philosophy and forces behind why the techniques work can help you to live a more examined life.

Of course, as with all tools and techniques, the ideas ahead can be used to live a dishonest, inauthentic, and manipulative life as well. In the final part of this book, my aim is to convince you to follow the nobler path. That, I believe, is the best way to improve your financial fortunes and help you live a better life.

And that, to me, is quite Taoist.

FOREWORD
BY CHRISTOPHER L. FUSSELL

When I first met John Kim, we fought. That's not a metaphor. This fight wasn't a misunderstanding. It was deliberate. Within minutes of shaking hands, we were on the mat, grappling.

A mutual friend had brought us together to explore a long-term business idea. In preparation for the day, this friend had asked, "What should we do in the morning to get to know each other better?"

Now, there are countless boring, traditional ways to answer that question—coffee, golf, a whiteboard conversation. But our mutual friend was a black belt in jiu jitsu. John, I'd been told, trained regularly and had earned his purple belt. I'd spent much of my early life wrestling and picked up enough jiu jitsu while in the SEAL teams to know how humbling the sport can be. So, I offered something a little different to my friend: "Let's find a gym and roll."

In my experience, there's no better way to get to know someone than through a controlled fight. Rolling with another person, you can sense a lot about them. Are they nervous or calm? Rigid or fluid? When do they exert, and when do they relax?

I knew walking in that I was the least experienced of the three, but that was the point. I've long believed that one of the clearest ways to read someone is to meet them in a low-risk domain where they clearly hold the advantage. When someone has the upper hand—physical, intellectual, financial—how do they behave? Do they use it to dominate? Do they retreat into performative humility? Or do they meet you where you are and see if something real can be built? Are they a student of life, seeing everyone and every moment as a chance to explore and learn?

That morning on the mats, I saw quickly who John really was. He flowed. He tested. He smiled when things got tough. He offered just enough resistance to stretch my limits, and just enough grace to let me find a path. There was no performative toughness, no ego. Just clarity. Control. Joy.

The best fighters—and the best leaders—don't need to show you they're in charge. They already know that. Instead, they want to build a relationship based on trust and understanding. We had bigger things to accomplish—our morning workout was just a step on the path.

Later that afternoon, John asked me about my own journey—from the SEAL teams into the world of leadership consulting and business transformation. It was, not surprisingly, a nonobvious move to him.

"Well," I said, "counterterrorism, in the end, is really about people. Not just individuals, but the stories they're telling themselves, and the world they see from a perspective that is their own. The societal myths that shaped them. No one's born a terrorist—just like no one's born a Navy SEAL. We're all the product of stories. Some stories take people toward violence. Mine took me toward service.

"When those stories collide," I continued, "you have to find a way to bring them to a close—to write a final chapter that lets the world move on. Oddly enough, consulting is not that different. You can't help a team or a company until you understand the narrative they're living in—and the future chapters they're trying to write for their business."

I was riffing, but I could see John listening intently. What I didn't realize at the time was that I'd walked right into one of the central principles behind his life's work: the idea that capital, like conflict or change, moves through narrative. If you don't understand the story and the characters who control the capital, it will evade you forever. Someone else will write the final chapter, not you.

That moment sparked a long conversation. It was the first of many, and the start of an important friendship.

Fortunately for you, reader, John—or Kimmer to his friends—has laid his ideas out in the book you now hold.

The Tao of Fundraising is unlike anything I've read in the world of business or capital. It is part philosophical treatise, part tactical manual, and part personal code. It pulls from ancient wisdom and modern neuroscience, from Aristotle and Cialdini, from Buddhist detachment and high-stakes private equity. Despite the range, it holds together beautifully. Not as a loose collection of clever ideas—but as a *system* that you can adopt into your own life and way of thinking.

What John and his co-author, Seth Libby, have done here is extraordinary: They've mapped the invisible architecture behind fundraising—the terrain most people walk through blindly, often never seeing the *actual* game they are involved in as it unfolds around them. At its core, this book is not about pitch decks or financing terms or even money itself. It's about energy—how it flows between people, how it is built through attention and trust, and how it is either amplified or destroyed by safety or fear, clarity or misunderstanding.

The *Tao* they lay out is rooted in a truth that anyone who's ever had to lead under pressure comes to learn—people don't make decisions with their frontal lobes. Not at first, anyway. High-risk decisions come from the gut, the limbic system. This is home to our core identity, the place where our drive for stability and control is rooted. The story we tell ourselves *about ourselves* drives our instinctive reactions under pressure and stress. The mind often shows up later to rationalize what the body has already decided.

If you want to raise capital, you're not just asking for money. You're asking someone to feel safe with you. To want to be in your orbit. To believe—emotionally and cognitively—that your success is in their best interest.

That doesn't happen through facts alone. It happens through resonance. If you don't understand their story—and the role your character plays in that story—you won't be around for another scene, and you certainly won't gain any of their precious resources.

What makes this book so powerful is that it teaches the mechanics of that resonance without falling into manipulation. John doesn't just want you to be more effective—he wants you to be more *aware*. Of yourself and of others. Of power and how it's perceived. Of trust and the shadows that can distort it.

He shows you how to stoke desire, yes—but to do it ethically. He explores the theater of fundraising—what he calls "persona play"—but frames it not as a deception but as a form of deep empathy: meeting the person across the table in the language they understand, while remaining grounded in who you are.

He breaks down complex decision-making dynamics— tribal, meritocratic, monarchical—and explains how to tailor your pitch to the system you're walking into. He warns of the "Drama Triangle" of Hero, Villain, and Victim and shows how great fundraisers resist those roles, opting instead for co-creation.

And he does all of this while holding fast to a deeper truth: that fundraising is not just a tool for wealth accumulation. It is a path toward impactful living. A way of building, giving, and empowering. A force that, when wielded well, can serve causes far greater than the self.

But this book also knows and acknowledges the dark side. It doesn't pretend that influence is always used for good. It acknowledges that these tools—like any powerful art—can be abused. The same techniques that build trust can be weaponized. Charisma, if untethered from ethics, becomes manipulation.

That's why the Tao matters. Because without it, you're just performing. With it, you're building something real.

John doesn't want to teach you how to win a pitch. He wants to teach you how to carry yourself through the world—with clarity, with integrity, and with strength. He wants you to understand power—not to seek it blindly but to hold it wisely, in service of something meaningful.

In my own life, I've led teams in war zones and helped businesses navigate crisis. I now work at the edge of scientific discovery. Across every one of those domains—combat, capital, or cutting-edge R&D—the forces that govern behavior remain constant: fear, trust, ego, story.

This book speaks to all of them.

It's written for fundraisers, but it's just as useful for leaders, educators, creators, and anyone who seeks to move through the world with a little more control over their own story.

If you're holding this book, I assume you want to raise capital. You're in the right place.

But if you're willing to look deeper, *The Tao of Fundraising* will offer you something even more valuable:

A philosophy.

A mirror.

And a way forward.

You're lucky to have Kimmer as your guide. I'm lucky to call him my friend.

Now . . . step on the mat.

INTRODUCTION

Open any self-help book in the business section of your local bookshop, and somewhere within you'll find the same advice:

"Problems can't stop you. Only you can stop you."

"You're in control of your own destiny."

"Success is falling down nine times and standing up ten."

You hear that same advice in TED Talks and CEO interviews. It's the advice plastered across the covers of business magazines and guides on entrepreneurship.

It's all great advice. But it's pretty useless.

It's useless because it's all aspiration without any of the practical tools you need to actually accomplish it. In essence, it's advice that tells you to go it alone and walk away from the traditional hierarchies and systems that allow for steady, if unremarkable, advancement, without ever explaining how you're going to survive on your own.

It's like telling you to jump into the deep end before teaching you how to swim.

Most people would love to control their own destinies and pursue their own ambitions unimpeded by bureaucracies and management. That's why the advice is so appealing. These people remain stuck within the system not because they lack the right mindset but because they have no idea how to control the financial realities that control their lives. Without this control, the whole system is rigged to ensure the world happens *to* you, that others control your destiny, and that you always work for a boss.

The reason a chef works two shifts at someone else's restaurant instead of her own is the same reason a software developer stays in his role at Facebook instead of starting his own tech company. It's the same reason a modestly successful family business remains modest in size and doesn't scale. It all comes down to a lack of control over the money within the system.

The key to gaining that control is *fundraising*. It's only when you possess influence over the flow of capital—when you have the ability to acquire money by getting others to give it to you—that you can achieve the freedom to go out on your own and take control over your own destiny.

Essentially: *Without any money behind them, the best ideas remain just ideas.*

That's the nature of not just capitalism but humanity. Every system ever invented requires the ability to acquire large amounts of assets or money in order to spark new potential. Yet few places actually teach us how to do that. We don't instruct people on how important this is, let alone how to do it.

It's time to change that.

For almost everyone, the thing that will most directly and significantly change the probabilities of their success—the one factor that will provide people control of their own destiny—is the ability to acquire capital. If you want to be a leader, if you want to go out on your own, if you want to inspire people or change the world, you better be able to acquire resources.

Wrestling for Resources

Most of the time, people get things backward. They assume that all they need to take control of their destiny is to have one big idea. Once they have that big idea, they think the money will find them. But that's not reality. In truth, fundraising is a cage match between the person who needs the capital and the person who doesn't want to invest—with the latter holding almost all the power.

The question, then, is this: How do you win a fight when most of the power is on the other side?

To answer that, let's extend the metaphor. Imagine two people entering a fighting ring. On one side, you see a large man, six-foot-five, with broad, muscled shoulders and powerful arms. In the other, a much shorter, much less impressive-looking man. Who would you expect to win that fight?

Based solely on what you know so far, the answer is obvious: The larger man should win. All else being equal, size and strength will almost always determine victory. But all else in this fight is not equal. In this story, the smaller man possesses knowledge that the larger man does not. Unbeknownst to the larger man, the smaller man has spent his life studying multiple martial arts. The larger man has no such practice.

The difference in their knowledge completely changes the odds. When the bell rings and the two meet in the middle of the fighting circle, the larger man fights on instinct. He throws punches with all his muscle and weight behind him, but he throws them awkwardly, and to his surprise, the smaller man dodges and blocks them with ease before eventually grasping the larger man's outstretched arm, throwing him to the ground, and locking him in a position he cannot escape from.

The smaller man wins.

We might expect this. Most of us have seen a martial arts movie or two in which the master changes the odds through their skill. But this dynamic is true beyond fighting and cinema. It's also true in business and fundraising.

In business, money tends to stay put. It pools in the same places it has always resided—at the largest banks and with the wealthiest families. Those who control the resources are powerful, and they aren't eager to share. Ordinarily, we have no recourse to disrupt this situation. But just as a master of martial arts can dominate a much larger and stronger fighter, so too can a master of what I call the Tao of Fundraising flip the circumstance against even the most cynical and experienced allocator of capital.

A Multidisciplinary Art

"Tao" is an ancient Chinese word that often gets translated as "way" or "path." The term may share ancestry with similar words scattered across the Indo-European language family.[1] By following this "path," we are meant to live aligned with the natural forces of the universe. It also connects to the art of working within the harmony of these natural forces. The Tao of Fundraising is an extension of this concept. It involves aligning ourselves with the natural forces that guide our human and animal existence in our relationship with capital.

To align ourselves, we have to see the Tao (which will be our shorthand for the ideas of this book) as a sort of multidisciplinary art. Success in fundraising requires a nuanced understanding of multiple practices and philosophies, just as a film director must be a master of many skills to create a film. They must be a master of social interactions to get the most from their actors. They must be able to recognize good writing and craft some of it themselves. They need to understand what soundtrack would best communicate the emotion they want from a scene. They could use coding and digital skills to work more closely with their effects team. And that's all before we even get to the basics, like understanding sound, lighting, editing, and good acting.

This same reliance on multidisciplinary mastery is seen in mixed martial arts (MMA). A master of one martial art can greatly improve their odds in a fight, but limiting the understanding to that single style can also expose the master to risk. For example, while a jiu jitsu master may be able to grapple, flip, and lock down an opponent, they might struggle to counter a proficient boxer who can stay on their feet.

Fundraising is like this as well. When trying to secure funding, there are very few rules that everyone follows. Investors who are uncertain about your proposition and those competing for the same resources are always liable to seek out the weaknesses in your practice. They'll take any advantage if you leave yourself exposed.

To counter this possibility, you need a multidisciplinary approach, one that incorporates the techniques of many different schools. That's precisely what the Tao offers: a set of practices and insights from many different "schools" that prepare you for whatever is ahead. The Tao of Fundraising is assembled from thousands of years of thought on persuasion and best business practices. In this book, you will encounter schools of philosophy, psychology, economics, and sales. You will come across thoughts from ancient Greece, the Bible, traditional Buddhist dogma, early modern Poland, and twenty-first-century America. You'll read about ideas most commonly utilized by the best therapists and sales techniques taught in the top MBA programs.

While we'll touch on religion and morality in places, you don't have to share any particular faith or worldview to benefit from these teachings. For our purposes, the true value is in the tapestry of insights we can weave together from these concepts. All these practices come together to provide a powerful Tao that can enable anyone to build the necessary relationships and win the important arguments to raise the funds they need.

A Tao for the Novice and the Master

I was recently sitting down with a prominent CEO who runs a large corporation. She had asked to speak to me about a venture capital fund she wanted to start. I have known her for some time, and her reputation as a talented, intelligent, and driven leader is well-earned. She has succeeded at everything she's ever attempted.

It was no surprise, then, when she told me I was there simply to provide a little initial guidance. She expected she could raise the necessary capital without the help of a professional fundraiser. When I suggested it might not be quite that simple, she balked.

"Tell me," she said, "why can't I raise this fund?"

"It isn't that you can't do it," I answered. "It's that you may not understand all that is ahead. You have had a very successful career. But now you want to raise $500 million. That seems quite achievable relative to the challenges you've overcome in your career. And, frankly, it probably is achievable. But tell me, how many people do you think you would need to meet to hit your target?"

She hesitated. "Well, I just want to meet the five or ten investors who really understand what I am doing. They will give me the money I need."

Shaking my head, I said, "Everyone says they are just looking for the few people that 'get them.' But that's a little naive. You can reach a few people who want to support you. After all, you are a very successful person, and people really like you. However, if you are asking me for fundraising advice, it means that you don't know enough of those people. And investors who don't already have a relationship with you will not give you any special privilege. In other words, you are going to have to play the numbers game. So assuming that your average commitment will be

$10 million, which is quite large to begin with, and you are able to convert 20 percent of your meetings into investors, which is quite high relative to the market, then the math is that you need to meet with somewhere between two to three hundred investors."

She leaned forward a bit, her interest piqued, as I continued.

"And that, again, assumes you have an impressive *conversion ratio*. Because it's easy to meet people, but it takes a lot of calories to close them. Realistically, when you meet someone, if you're good at this, you have a 50 percent chance of getting a second meeting—if you're really good. After you get that second meeting, you have to prove to the investor that they should trust you with their money. That takes more meetings. Across those meetings, you'll have to build that trust and walk them through the complexities and their questions. All the while, they can drop out at any time for any reason. There are dozens of other people trying to get that same $10 million. Do you have the skills and the discipline necessary to deliver on that at least fifty times?"

Very quickly, she saw where I was heading. Fundraising isn't as easy as it might seem at first. But nor is it as impossible as it can feel to those who are unfamiliar with this world.

To harness the power of the Tao of Fundraising, you have to come to it with humility. Anyone who has had success in fundraising can always learn more and improve their technique. And those who have never fundraised can master it—but only if they accept the process associated with that mastery.

Success with the Tao comes down to how you approach it. Fundraising is more than an activity or career; it can be a way of living and experiencing life. The same principles are at work whether you're raising $500,000, $5 million, or even $1 billion. The number of investors changes, and the amount you ask for changes, but the principles remain the same.

Small or large, fundraising presents significant challenges that the Tao can help you overcome. The smaller the ask, the more likely you can find one person to cover all the funding—there are many people out there who can cut a small check. But the more you scale your "ask," the harder it becomes to find one investor to provide all the funding. At that point, you need the Tao to help you get to *yes* over and over again.

The principles of the Tao are valuable at any level of success and for any level of experience—and as with martial arts, greater knowledge leads to greater mastery. Graham Duncan, expert investor and co-founder of East Rock Capital, once brilliantly articulated this progression in an article titled "The Playing Field." Just as a novice begins karate or tae kwon do as a white belt and rises through the ranks to black, Duncan argued that career development has five similar stages of development:

1. Apprentice—learning the game
2. Expert—mastering the game you were taught

3. Professional—making the game you were taught fit your own strengths and weaknesses
4. Master—changing the game you play as part of your own self-expression and operating at scale
5. Steward—becoming part of the playing field itself and mentoring the next generation[2]

The longer a student of the Tao studies and practices, the greater their insights and the potential of their practice. The greater their potential, the further they can develop this path for themselves and for others.

The Road Ahead

This is a gateway book, and thus my aim is not to transform everyone into a master of fundraising. Instead, I hope to start each of you on your fundraising journey, introducing the key teachings you will need to develop, practice, and master if you wish to have more control over the resources you need to "be your own boss" or "control your own destiny." You must determine for yourself how far you take the Tao and how much you integrate it into your life. This book is a beginning, with an arrow pointing in the right direction. How far you follow it is entirely up to you.

With that in mind, remember that the "Tao" refers to the natural order of things—a philosophy that describes the character of the universe. That is the ultimate reason why this book exists. I am not revealing the Tao to make people rich—although I expect that to be a by-product. I have written all that follows because these ideas are simply true of our financial system, our human interactions, and our relationship with money and economics. As the saying goes, "It is what it is," and I want others to understand what "it" is.

For some reason, this focus is extremely rare in business literature today. Capital formation is very important for our system, our companies, and our individual careers . . . but who is teaching us how to actually raise capital? Experts talk about how to use it and how to invest it. Thousands of books have been written, and whole business schools have been founded, on these subjects, but no one talks about how we get capital in the first place. No one tells us how to go out and get the money we need to do the other things they recommend. The money is assumed, even though very few of us can make that assumption.

This is a shame not just because of the constraints it places on entrepreneurs and established companies, but because the Tao of Fundraising offers a path to more than monetary riches. It can lead to a richer life. Through the Tao, we can better understand our relationships, our responsibilities, and the systems we otherwise unwittingly take part in—and we can better control our role in each. Following the Tao will undoubtedly make you a better friend, a more inspirational leader, or a more successful entrepreneur, because it will give you clarity on how others think and how the world works.

Through the Tao, you'll understand what those in your life need psychologically when they are facing doubt, the philosophy behind Warren Buffett's wildly successful investments, and the reason Apple's designs remain the best and most innovative in the world today. And through that knowledge, you will be able to better live up to your potential. Instead of relying on a raw, subconscious understanding in every area of your life, you will be able to use these tools mindfully. Just as a master of martial arts can rely on technique instead of brute force—and therefore defend himself far more successfully—you will be able to consciously apply the principles of fundraising across your entire life to far greater effect.

Like any good philosophy, the Tao offers clarity on how the world works and our place in it—but perhaps surprisingly, it is also unique in how much it centers on empathy and the experiences of other people. Most philosophies of life focus on *me* and how *I* experience the world. The Tao of Fundraising considers the other person first. To be successful in fundraising, you must focus on the needs of the other person in the room. This has profound implications across all aspects of life.

As we move through this book and discuss the practical benefits of fundraising, the science and business practices behind it, and the tools of persuasion necessary to "win" investment, keep these additional benefits in mind. The Tao is more than a playbook for filling coffers; it's a more meaningful way of approaching life.

I know how extensive the potential of the Tao is because I have been developing and practicing it for decades. While I only ever made it to a purple belt in jiu jitsu, I believe I am a black belt in the Tao of Fundraising. I have used these techniques to raise more than $70 billion in private equity and venture capital. I have used them to cultivate relationships with people in my private and professional life. And I have used them to achieve purpose throughout my life.

This book represents an opportunity to share what I wish I'd known decades earlier. If I could go back thirty-five years and present this book to myself, I would be many years further ahead in my career, and I would have found equanimity much sooner in my life. I wish to offer that to you.

That is not to say that the journey is easy. Ask any martial arts or spiritual master, and they will tell you there is always much work required to become a steward of their discipline. But if you approach all that is ahead with a willingness to learn and a level of empathy that allows you to truly connect with others, the Tao can unlock unlimited rewards for all who follow it.

PART ONE

The Fundamentals

Chapter 1

The Power of Money

The world of feudal Japan was extremely hierarchical. At the top, you had the emperor, who was the source of all power (at least in theory). At the bottom, you had the vast majority of people who made up the peasants, artisans, and merchants who created all the resources for the kingdom.

Between these extremes is where it gets most interesting. Below the emperor were the kuge, who made up a small noble class, and the *shoguns*, who were the military leaders and true power of the country. Below the shoguns were the *daimyo*, the lords who owned large areas of land. The daimyo were protected by the *samurai*, who acted as their military force and protection.

And then there were the *rōnin*—traveling samurai who had no allegiance to a lord.

This system worked much like the medieval European version of feudalism you probably learned about in school. The lords sat at the top in their castles, collecting all the resources. The peasants did all the work and paid a huge portion of their labor to the lords in exchange for protection. The samurai acted much like knights, earning a place at the lord's table but sitting below them in stature.

To put this in stark economic terms, the farther up the pyramid you go, the more the resources "pool" together. The lower down the pyramid you go, the more people work to provide those resources for less and less reward.

When I put it that way, perhaps you can see how little has really changed. We have a very different kind of system now, a capitalist one, but the structure is not so different. Those at the top have most of the resources. That's why they're at the top. Those at the bottom do most of the work for the least reward. And those in the middle tend to advance through the useful skills they can offer their "lords." Today, we might look more for skill in writing code than handling a blade, but the principle still applies.

And yet, two groups in that pyramid stand out as unique: the samurai and rōnin. The samurai could rise to be among the true elites. They were granted land, wealth, prestige, and power based partly on skill. And though it was rare, occasionally someone from the lower castes could rise to become a samurai.

The rōnin followed a different path. They were able to go out on their own, live by their own code, and, to some extent, create their own fortune. They could choose to serve a new master or become wandering mercenaries.

The path of the rōnin was not an easy one. It was seen as shameful by the higher classes, which aimed to reduce opportunities for the rōnin. Yet rōnin could still survive because they had the necessary skills to do so.

Most likely, you are not part of the modern versions of the imperial, kuge, or shogun classes. Statistically, you are unlikely to have been born with enormous resources. To rise in this society, therefore, you have to become the equivalent of either a samurai or a rōnin. You either need to help accrue resources for a daimyo above you or find a way to build them up yourself. And that requires a deeper understanding of the nature of our system and how resources flow through it.

Ideas Need Funding

Many erroneously assume that the key to moving up through our system requires great ideas. They see ideas as the path to acquiring resources and scaling that pyramid to become daimyos in their own right. Obviously, a great idea helps make that possible, but it isn't actually the key to gaining those resources.

Great ideas are often floating in the air, and several perceptive individuals pick them up around the same time. Nikola Tesla and Thomas Edison famously disputed who invented the best form of electrical transmission. Isaac Newton and Gottfried Leibniz both demanded credit for inventing calculus. The winner in these battles is rarely determined by whose idea is better or whose idea came first. It usually comes down to who had access to power and money.

No one exemplifies this fact quite like my friend Aaron, whom I met in graduate school. Aaron is perhaps the most forward-thinking individual I know. After we graduated, he decided not to go into consulting or to Wall Street like the rest of us. Instead, he wanted to pursue an idea he'd had to transform the market. He foresaw a world in which the majority of books and music were sold online. This was the 1990s, and the idea seemed far-fetched to most. Not to everyone, though: Jeff Bezos was thinking the same thing. Aaron could never raise enough money to realize his idea at scale. That's what determined his outcome, not the quality of his idea. Eventually, Amazon put him out of business.

Not one to be deterred, Aaron had another big idea. In the early 2000s, he realized that internet and video technology were evolving at such a fast rate that people would soon be able to upload their videos and let everyone in the world watch them. Again, he couldn't secure funding. The founders of YouTube were much more successful at that.

His next idea was cannabis farming, just as laws were beginning to change. When he struggled to find the funding to scale, he moved on to vertical farming. It was the perfect way to grow enough food for a huge population while space was becoming more scarce. Once again, he couldn't convince anyone with significant capital to believe in his vision. Today, vertical farming has immense growth potential. His latest idea involves the use of microdoses of psilocybin and MDMA to help treat trauma. The technique isn't legal yet, but he's confident that the growing body of research will eventually force the law to change, leading to a huge new industry.

You'll never guess why he's struggling to get to the fore-front of that industry.

My friend is a genius. He's a visionary who's been proven right over and over again. But you have never heard of him or his companies because he hasn't been able to attract capital. And when you can't attract capital, it doesn't matter how good your ideas are.

Capital-ism

The story we tell ourselves about our economic system is a story of ideas. We talk about Henry Ford and Steve Jobs—people who had big ideas that changed the world. Capitalism, we say, is a system that allows great ideas to rise to the top and money to flow through them.

This is wrong. After all, our system is not called *idealism*; it's called *capitalism*. And *capital*-ism is, at its very root, an economic system built on accruing *capital* to make progress on ideas. The capital fuels ideas; the ideas don't fuel capital.

Again, this is not so different from feudalism. In a feudal system, those at the top control all the resources while those below do the work that creates those resources. The shoguns and daimyos of this world have never been particularly eager to hand over those resources. They do so only when someone proves they can provide real value. That's still the perception of capitalistic investors today.

There are many strengths and weaknesses within this system, but, ultimately, it is the one we have. *It is what it is*, as they say. In this system, the people who succeed most are those who are best able to convince the small number of people who control most of the capital to hand it over.

To put it as bluntly as possible, investors would rather invest their money in a mediocre idea with lots of money behind it than a great idea with no backers. It's simply a better bet.

While you may not like that reality, that's how the system works. So if you want to accomplish anything of significance, you'll have to learn to work within those constraints.

Capital Follows the Path of Least Resistance

One reason we have so much income inequality in our society is that capital almost always finds people who already have access to it. In feudal Japan, resources almost never left the palaces where the emperor, kuge, shoguns, and daimyos resided. Only those with access to the palace, such as the samurai, were ever likely to receive some of those resources.

Today, the social structure looks different, but the same principle holds true. It's easier to give rich, established people money because they're already in the room with capital. They know the people with capital. Their parents knew the people with capital. They have a good reputation with institutions with capital. And people give money to people they know.

Just as both running water and electricity flow along the path of least resistance, so do money and power. And the path of least resistance tends to run toward those who already have capital and people who know those who have capital. Capital exists in lots of places—in banks, in funds, with individual investors—but it all swirls around the same locations and among the same people.

As someone who went to Harvard Business School, I can tell you that the real value of an Ivy League education isn't the education itself. Today, many state schools can offer an education just as good as that of Yale or Brown (my undergraduate alma mater). Indeed, with vast online resources available, an enterprising self-taught person in Dubuque, Iowa could learn just as much as a registered student in Cambridge, Massachusetts. So no, the value of an Ivy League school is not in the quality of the instruction; the real advantage is the opportunity to connect with those who have capital and who will attract capital in their work.

Karl Alexander, Doris Entwisle, and Linda Olson, in their book *The Long Shadow*, found that the most important determinants of success on any basis—be it wealth, happiness, or possessions—are the parents you're born to, the place you're born, and the local resources of that area. It's all about who you know.[3]

This isn't much solace to those who were not born into wealthy families or who didn't attend Harvard. Luckily, there are ways to change the direction capital is flowing. Capital formation doesn't have to happen *to* you; it can happen *by* you—if you possess the right knowledge and skills.

What's Your Question?

In the capitalist system, the classic joke is, "We know the answer is money. But what is the question?"

The question is different for each person.

You are here because more money would make a difference in what you are seeking. Perhaps you want to design clothes and open an e-commerce business. Perhaps you want to raise $10 million to start a charity that provides assistance to a neglected community in need of help. Or perhaps you want to raise $100 million to develop a game-changing product at your Fortune 500 company.

Whatever your specific question is in this context, money is the answer. We often say that money is the root of all evil, but that's not true. (In point of fact, the origin for that saying, the Bible, actually called the *love* of money evil, not money itself.) Money is where all ambitions take root—the good and the bad. Money is the soil that provides the nutrients necessary for growth.

Some seeds require minimal fertilizer. A small business might need no more than an investment of tens of thousands of dollars to start showing green shoots. Others require far more. Moderna ran up a $1.5 billion deficit before inventing a Covid vaccine that helped save the world.[4] In each case, though, fertile soil is required to grow the opportunity, and you are tasked with finding it.

In the parable of the sower in the Gospel of Matthew, a farmer scatters seeds across his land. Some seeds land on the path and get eaten by birds, and some land in shallow soil or in a thorny patch and shrivel quickly. But a handful of seed lands in good earth and "produces a crop, yielding hundred, sixty or thirty times what was sown" (Matthew 13:23 NIV).

In the parable, the quality of the seeds is not important. It's the soil they land in that makes the difference. When a seed lands in the right soil, it can produce unbelievable bounty. When it doesn't, that seed's potential can never be realized.

In other words, a great seed, like a great idea, isn't enough. You have to pair it with the nutrient-rich soil of capital for it to grow. Whatever your ambitions—whatever your "question"—attracting funding is essential. Otherwise, you're just scattering your seed across the rocky ground and hoping it somehow takes root.

The Wealth Pyramid

Like feudal Japan, modern capitalism has its own wealth pyramid. And just like feudal Japan, resources play a different role depending on where you are in that pyramid.

Our modern wealth pyramid includes four different sections, each decreasing in size and increasing in access to resources as you move up. So far, this is similar to the feudal model, but here is where things have evolved over the centuries. The higher you climb up the pyramid, the greater you experience risk and the potential for gains. In the feudal system, those at the top had little to risk. They didn't really invest in anything other than protection through force. That's not the case at the top these days, as we'll see.

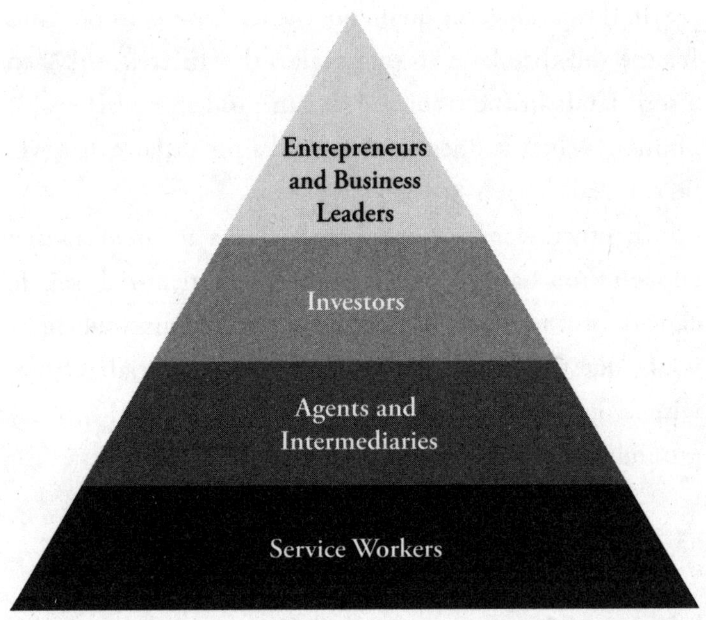

Level 1: Service Workers

Let's start at the bottom of our modern-day pyramid. This is where you find all the services that fuel our economy. These days, most people in developed economies are not peasant farmers. Instead, they provide some kind of service. Capitalism is a combination of capital and labor, and this is where most of the labor takes place. In fact, every business has at least some service component to it. This is the foundation of everything in our economy.

The service block includes everyone from restaurant waiters to pilots, from plumbers to professional athletes. Generally, in service, the greater the demand for the service and the greater the skill, the more an individual can earn.

An experienced software engineer can make hundreds of thousands of dollars a year because they have a skill that is in demand. The most popular musicians can earn millions on a concert tour, and a famous actor can command tens of millions for a single role for the same reasons. In the Bahamas, after a hurricane, experienced construction workers can charge a premium price because there's a huge need for their skill set. At other times, they make much less.

This is the level with the least capital risk. After all, a service provider does not have to invest any of their own money to make a profit. They find a company, get the job, and get paid. But this block also has the lowest ceiling for income.

Don't get me wrong. The ceiling is very high compared to the median American income. As noted above, it can range into the tens of millions—the sort of money the most famous and successful athletes and artists can make. But for the vast majority of people, the earnings potential is much lower than those in elite service roles.

For this very reason, additional resources are obviously much appreciated by the average individual in the service sector, but from an investment perspective, capital doesn't do much good. If you give more money to an electrician, they'll buy a new set of tools or a new truck, which might slightly increase their ability to service more houses—but only marginally. In this way, it isn't so different from how a lord might treat the peasants on their land. There was no good financial incentive to provide extra resources.

The only way for capital to play a larger role is for service workers to become entrepreneurs, a possibility we'll explore when we reach the top of the pyramid. Before we get to entrepreneurship, though, we have two other blocks in the middle of the pyramid.

Level 2: Agents and Intermediaries

Agents and intermediaries include salespeople of all sorts as well as fundraisers and brokers. These are the individuals who pair others with products or bring resources together. They connect people to other people, or people to something they want. Agents and intermediaries make more money than the service provider as a category (though not necessarily on an individual basis) because they can scale through commission. Essentially, they can sell over and over again. They can also scale the size of their sales or the size of their commission. Investment bankers work with billions of dollars and can make far more simply because they take a fraction of each investment.

Here, capital can be far more useful. The more access to capital, the bigger the commission. That's the nature of wealth creation: You can make far more as an agent or intermediary, even if the work is less valuable than the work of many service providers. The risk here is slightly higher, though. While in service, it all comes down to your skill—which, on some level, you control, as an agent or intermediary, your success also depends on the quality of the product you sell or the size of your commission. If the product doesn't attract buyers or the commission is too low, no amount of work will earn you enough to put food on the table.

Level 3: Investors

Above agents and intermediaries are the investors. Investors control the capital. This is the group you aim to provide access to fertile ground for your seeds. And that's a tough sell because there is a lot of risk at this level of the pyramid.

It's extremely hard to make money as an investor. You have to outperform the market—no easy feat. The more capital you have to invest, the greater your potential returns—but also the greater your exposure to risk. More often than not, the hope is to preserve the capital (or perform well enough so the capital providers won't find someone else to invest their money). But because of the potential upside to a big investment, investors sometimes need only a few wins to secure massive returns.

Level 4: Entrepreneurs and Business Leaders

Above investors are only entrepreneurs and business leaders, who sit at the top of the pyramid. Here, the risk and potential are highest. It's hard to succeed at this level, but if you do, you get to keep all the money—and the rewards can be gigantic. We know the names of many of the greatest successes at this level: Jeff Bezos, Bill Gates, Elon Musk, the Walton family, the Hewlett and Packard families, Michael Bloomberg, and so on.

This is the level where capital can be the most effective—where it can be consumed and transformed into value, ideally for everyone in society.

Fundraising's effectiveness varies wildly depending on where your question places you on this pyramid. For those in the service strata who wish to remain in it, capital can only modestly improve things. The further up the pyramid you go, the more potential capital you can unlock.

The commercial ideas you will encounter in this book will speak most directly to the intermediaries (Level 2). I am, after all, a fundraiser myself, and for those who wish to become fundraisers, this book will show how you can apply this practice at an exquisite level. However, investors and entrepreneurs will also find much ahead that helps them better understand their roles in our system.

Ultimately, the real value of this book is that it will describe things as they are—whether it is capital's role within our system or the pattern every successful conversation follows. That is what the Tao of Fundraising can provide: a clearer understanding of how our financial world works and what we can do to ensure capital formation happens *by* us instead of *to* us.

It's the same principles that have always been in play, the same tools that worked as well in feudal Japan as they do today.

Chapter 2

The Fundamentals
of Fundraising

Sun Tzu claimed to be able to determine who would win a battle based on their calculations and preparations.[5] He certainly would have been able to predict the winner in the battle between David and Goliath.

While the Bible positions this clash as a battle over control of the Holy Land, we can understand it a different way. This was a fight for resources. The Holy Land rests in a prized position on the map, between the powers of Mesopotamia and Egypt. It has excellent farmland and access to the sea.

In political terms, these were two warring minor regional powers vying for control over the resources that could make their people rich. But of those two minor powers, one clearly had the advantage. In the book of Exodus, we're told the Israelites avoided the Philistines when leaving Egypt because facing them would mean war—and the Israelites would end up returning to Egypt.[6]

But we don't need to gaze that far back to see the Philistine advantage: Simply look at Goliath, who was so imposing and powerful that no Israelite dared face him. This makes it all the more remarkable that David not only won but that, despite all appearances, the young shepherd had every advantage.

According to the Bible, David knew he was going to win the battle because "the LORD who delivered me from the paw of the lion and from the paw of the bear will deliver me from the hand of this Philistine" (1 Samuel 17:37 ESV). The text is clear: David believed God was on his side, so there was no question who was going to come away victorious.

But David didn't actually need God to win. Malcolm Gladwell famously made the argument in his book *David and Goliath* that David had all the advantages even without divine support.[7] Even though David was smaller, younger, and untrained in close combat, science was on his side.

Similar to our big-man-versus-smaller-man example in this book's introduction, David had the right weapon and the right experience for the type of fight he was entering. Goliath had the strength and experience for a close, face-to-face brawl, but with a rock and his sling, David was a sniper. With Goliath standing at a distance, David could win by launching stones from that sling before the first blow was struck. Facing those dynamics, Goliath's size actually worked against him. It just made him a bigger, easier target.

When you see it that way, far from being the overwhelming favorite in the fight, Goliath had everything going against him. You just needed to know how to attack him. That isn't speculation or spirituality; it's scientific truth.

Equally, Goliath could have reduced these advantages. He could have used a shield. He could have specified that the battle must be fought hand to hand. But because David better understood the nature of the fight, he walked into war almost certain of victory. We know David must have recognized this in advance because he stepped onto the battlefield without any armor at all. David was confident Goliath would be dead long before the Philistine could lay a hand upon the future Israelite king.

This holds true in fundraising as well. In any market, there will almost always be a Goliath who's already established. They're the big competition that has all the money and all the investors. In order for you, a modern-day David, to overcome that limitation, you have to use the laws of fundraising to your advantage. Likewise, if a Goliath wishes to remain in charge, they have to use those same laws to maintain their power.

If you know the nature of the interaction ahead of you and what is required for victory from the outset, you have all the advantages necessary to win the investment before even walking into the room—no matter how big the Goliath is in your town.

Fundraising Is Built on Principles

Like all great philosophies, there is an intersection between the Tao and science. The Tao is built on what we know is true of business, human interactions, and psychology. It is built on an understanding of *what is*.

In David's story, the author tells us that David's first principle was the knowledge that God was on his side. But his second principle was pretty important too: the knowledge that size matters in close combat but not at a distance.

Without understanding these two principles, David never would have had the courage and conviction to face the giant and beat him.

The fundraising world is full of Goliaths who can easily raise money. Of course they can. Few people would be willing to say no to Jeff Bezos or Elon Musk. But you can be small and mighty in this field if you understand the Tao from the ground up.

At the foundation of the Tao of Fundraising are five principles:

1. The necessity of preparation
2. The role our animalistic traits play in decision-making
3. The paradox of control
4. The relationship of trust, demand, and attention
5. The basic components of the fundraising process

To truly understand fundraising, you must start here. So let's look more closely at each of those five essential fundraising factors.

Principle 1: Prepare and Plan

The first law of fundraising can be stated in three words: *Preparation is everything*. Better preparation and training vastly increase the likelihood of your victory. Like David before Goliath, if you know what you are up against, you can counter it and achieve success. And as I've already said, the same would have gone for Goliath as well. If you know who's going to invest, where to find them, and what you need to say to convince them, then you'll know what it will take to complete the deal.

If you seek investment without preparation, you're relying on luck and assumption. This is precisely what Goliath did. He assumed that because of his size and because he "had been a warrior from his youth," as the Bible says,[8] he could see off any challenge. When it really counted, he got it wrong.

Fundraising is a funny activity. It's one of the few high-stakes activities that people jump into with absolutely no training. Can you imagine a doctor or a pilot saying to you, "Don't worry. I've never done this before, but I should be able to pull this off. How hard can it be?"

In reality, there's little room for unpreparedness in the world of fundraising. Just like a doctor or a pilot, if you don't have any training, the probability of success is very low. The reality is that the investors you will be speaking to have probably been making investment decisions for years. They also probably already have relationships with the Goliaths in the area. So, in order to even the odds, you need to use the same advantages David did. You need to know the rules of combat better than the investor so you can "appear where you are not expected."[9]

Principle 2: Humans Are Animals Too

To understand all the ideas ahead, you have to accept that humans are animals. The ways we encounter the world, the ways we respond and interact, and the ways we make decisions all stem from a basic animalistic survival framework. We happen to be unique in that we have a frontal lobe that gives these instincts meaning, but at their root, our basic instincts look very similar to other animals we share the planet with.

Essentially, investors, like everyone else, make choices about where to invest mostly through emotion and instinct. Sure, logic plays a role, but it's much smaller than what we generally assume.

When we strip away our egos and seek wisdom from the animal world, we can discover deeper truths about ourselves and those we aim to convince to hand over their money.

Principle 3: The Uncertainty Paradox

Within the act of fundraising, there is an innate paradox that you simply must accept if you want to have success within the field. Here's the paradox in its simplest form: *We enter fundraising to gain control; but to fundraise we must accept that we have no control.*

Digging in, this uncertainty paradox states that we all want control over our lives. This is the reason we're so attracted to those self-help books that tell us we can have control simply by changing our mindset. But that control is possible only if we have control over the resources we need. We must control enough resources to open our business, to invest in our research, or to market our brilliant idea.

To gain this control, you must enter a very uncertain process, hence the paradox. As a fundraiser, you are required to enter rooms where you have little, if any, power. The people who have the resources are in control. They can pull out of a deal at any time. You can do everything right—adhere to all the advice that follows—and still fail.

Uncertainty is the greatest frustration within the fundraising process. To embrace this journey, you have to embrace the fact that it isn't like a race in which the fastest always wins or a chess game in which the best player usually wins. It's more akin to hunting and gathering: You do everything you can to put yourself in the best situation to kill your prey or to find the best berries. You read the tracks on the ground, learn the behavior of the animals, and remember markers of edible vegetation. But you still often end up coming home empty-handed.

No matter how good you are, there will be times you don't succeed. Understanding this principle is the only way forward. As my good friend Jim Dethmer once said, "The antidote to fear isn't courage. It's acceptance."[10]

Most people struggle to accept this paradox, and that lack of acceptance leads to failure. Either they try to force control into the process or the lack of control in fundraising turns them to other processes that are doomed to fail. The result? They gain neither the capital they need nor the control they want.

In order to get control, you have to be willing to give up control. It's as simple as that.

Principle 4: The Atomic Reaction of Fundraising

$$Trust \cap Demand \cap Attention = Energy$$

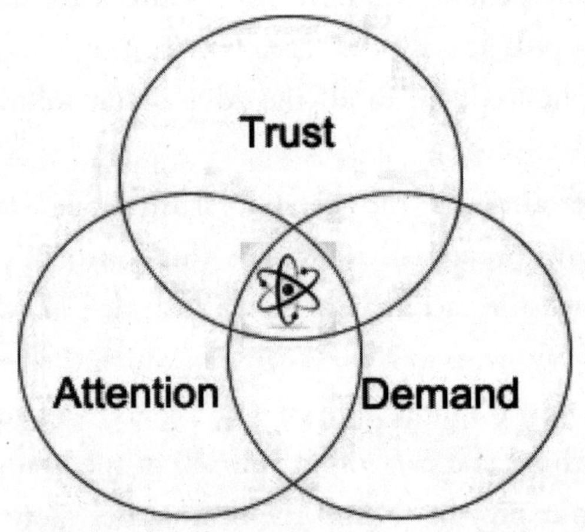

An atomic reaction unleashes an immense amount of energy into the world. When used with expertise, it can fuel a whole city. An atomic reaction in fundraising can be equally powerful—bringing together billions of dollars to fuel ideas that will change humanity. Creating such a financial reaction, whether enormous or much smaller in scale, requires the combination of three elements: one part *demand*, one part *attention*, and one part *trust*. When those three elements come together, the reaction can be spectacular.

This reaction doesn't just hold for fundraising; it's true of every sale. Whatever you want to sell—whether it's a fund, an app, toothpaste, or T-shirts—people have to trust you, they have to want what you're selling, and they have to pay attention long enough to realize that you have what they want.

Consider how cereal companies convince customers to buy their product in the grocery store. They strategically use your shopping experience to get a box of their breakfast food into your cart.

First, these companies know that every person who steers a cart into the cereal aisle has at least a *latent demand* for their product. After all, most people eat breakfast, and most cereal aisles are devoted almost exclusively to cereals and other breakfast items. So, if you're in the aisle, they think you're probably looking for something to eat for breakfast.

But that isn't enough to ensure a sale. You could choose any cereal in that aisle. So, second, they need your *attention*.

Famously, the sugary cereal options are placed at eye level of children. The boxes are also brightly colored with cartoon characters on the front. More "grown-up" cereals are often found on higher shelves, featuring duller colors and a basic picture of the cereal on the front.

Now that they've caught your eye, the third and final thing they need is for you to *trust* them. To earn that trust, cereal companies rely on the goodwill their brands have built up over decades of providing you with an enjoyable breakfast. You've liked Kellogg's cereal since you ate Frosted

Flakes as a child. You trust Kellogg's to offer an adult cereal that you'll equally love.

Combine all three elements successfully—demand, attention, and trust—and Kellogg's has a sale.

Politicians work with these same elements in their efforts to get elected. They run commercials to get your attention and have events where they give away a free meal to get you to listen to their stump speech. Once you're there, they sell you on all the things they think you (demand). Whatever the core issues of that election, they tell you they'll guarantee the results you desire if you vote for them. All that's left is earning your trust, which is why they spend so much time in their speech trying to convince you that they're an average American just like you. They tell their story in such a way that they (ideally, at least) become relatable and likable. Then they talk about all the institutions and individuals who have endorsed them. All of this builds a sense of trust.

Many have argued that the result of the 2016 election came down to trust. The electorate simply didn't trust Hillary Clinton—who was undeniably the more experienced candidate—and that cost her enough votes that Donald Trump became president.

These same dynamics are in play in fundraising. In order to fund any project, you must have a product that interests the investor (demand), the means to get and hold their interest (attention), and the credibility to live up to your promises (trust).

Those are the raw elements involved in every reaction that transfers dollars from their pocket to your fund.

Principle 5: The Fundraising Formula

**Pipeline x Conversion Rate x
Bite Size = Fundraising**

The fundraising formula above outlines the crucial elements and central process required to secure an investment from an individual. Every fundraise has three factors at play:

1. **Pipeline:** The pool of people who might consider investing
2. **Conversion Rate:** The percentage of prospects who say yes
3. **Bite Size:** The amount each investor is willing to put into your fund

This equation creates a natural set of trade-offs for every fundraiser. You can have fewer people in your pipeline if you convert at a high rate. You can also have fewer people and convert at a lower rate if the bite size is larger. If the bite size is small and the conversion rate is low, you need an enormous pipeline—and probably a lot of time.

Unless you have a truly exceptional product—say, Nvidia raising money for the next generation of processors—you can't have everything your way. So, how are you going to balance those three factors to reach the funding amount you need?

This law may seem simple, but its nuances are often hard to grasp even for experienced fundraisers in the field. Just this morning, I spoke to a venture capital group raising a new fund. They were confident they had their formula right. They had a sizable pipeline, and they were converting

80 percent of their first meetings into second meetings. But they were closing only 10 percent of those second meetings at the bite size they were looking for. Essentially, they confused the interest within their pipeline for conversion into actual funding.

Based on their flawed math, their first question to me was "Can you help us meet more people?"

"Do you really think that's what your problem is?" I asked them. They looked at me with a mix of shock and bewilderment. I let them consider the question a moment before explaining, "Your problem isn't how many people you're talking to. Your problem is the percentage of people who take the second meeting but don't close."

The easiest solution for them was to improve that conversion rate. Somewhere between that first meeting and the end of the second one, something was breaking down in the fundraising atomic reaction. Were they not building enough trust? Were they not convincing investors this was something they really wanted? Was someone else in the same space competing for the investor's attention?

If they could solve that, the fund would grow to the size they needed.

Fundraising Requires More Than Principles

To best Goliath, David needed more than confidence and a knowledge of the principles of warfare. Such understanding could only benefit him because he already had another form of knowledge—namely, how to use his slingshot with expert precision.

In the same way, the information in this chapter is entirely academic until you learn how to use the tools that allow you to take advantage of these principles. Those tools include certain skills we will cover in the second part of this book. But they equally include an awareness of the laws of the fundraising universe.

To put this in terms of David's story, he needed the skill to use the sling, but he also needed an innate understanding of how the laws of motion work. Use enough force over the right distance, and the rock he flung at Goliath would kill him. Only with that knowledge could he utilize the skills he'd developed over his young life.

For the fundraiser, the skills of persuasion we will cover in part 2 will be useful only if they first understand the laws that govern fundraising.

Chapter 3

The Laws of Fundraising

Somewhere around the year AD 300, the mystic Zosimos of Panopolis discussed a process he believed was ancient and supernatural: the ability to transform lead into the most precious metal of all, gold. The value of such a process would be immense. Zosimos felt it was a key connection to the divine. On a more practical level, it represented a pathway to collecting immense resources for any who could crack the code.

Unfortunately, the tools available to Zosimos were not up to the task of creating what became known as the "philosopher's stone." He only had the ideas of alchemy to work with, a rudimentary conception of the nature of elements. Alchemy as a concept can be found in many ancient cultures, but it has limited connection to how the material world actually behaves—as evidenced by the fruitless efforts of generation after generation to achieve the philosopher's stone.

From late antiquity to the late Middle Ages—from Egypt to Greece to the Islamic caliphate—many great minds attempted to transmute lead into gold, all to no avail.

This wasn't because those making such efforts were fools. They simply lacked an understanding of the laws of the universe that could explain why they couldn't achieve their aim.

For that, they would need a new science: chemistry. Coming out of the Enlightenment, chemistry offered an explanation for the building blocks of the material world. It more accurately explained *what is*. Through this science, it would eventually become clear that the reason alchemists kept failing was because lead had eighty-two protons in its nucleus compared to gold's seventy-nine. Fundamentally changing these elements would require more than an ancient misunderstanding of chemical reactions.

But that didn't mean it was impossible. In the past hundred years or so, scientists have in fact been able to transmute other metals into gold. The process is complex and expensive—and therefore not the hoped-for straightforward path to resources—but it was proved possible because they were working with the true laws of chemistry.

The Law of Differentiation

(Track Record + Differentiation)/ Complexity of Story

The principles we covered at the end of the last chapter were high-level and general. They referred to *what fundraising is*. From here on, we'll introduce formulas that nuance our practice. Up first is the *Law of Differentiation*. Essentially, this law tells you how to take the attention you earn and show investors that you are *the* person with *the* product worthy of their investment dollars.

In order to convince anyone to give you money, you have to be the better, more trustworthy, more attractive offer, thereby enticing investors to pay attention and pick you over the reigning heavyweight.

So, what makes you different? In what way do you stand apart?

This is where the Law of Differentiation comes into play.

You start with the first factor in the equation: your *track record*. Your track record is the shortest route to increasing trust with an investor and attracting their interest. Much of my own ability to raise funds comes from the fact that I have successfully done it so many times over the past four decades. Investors know they can trust me to do it again. If I reach out to them, most of them are going to respond and ask for details.

If, for example, you are seeking an investment to build a series of gas stations across the Midwest, having successfully built gas stations in the past is going to make a huge difference. It lowers the risk for the investor.

Of course, this is an advantage only if you have a track record in this specific area. Having general investment experience or experience in a related area isn't going to convince hardy, seasoned investors. In other words, if you've only ever *managed* a gas station, you can't gain trust that you know how to *build* and *own* a gas station. That experience doesn't improve your track record.

A thin track record can at times be overcome with performance. If you have earned a lot of return for investors already, others will come to trust that you know what you're doing.

However, this isn't always the case. Sometimes you have no choice but to start from zero—without a track record or strong performance. This is where the second factor in the Law of Differentiation formula, *differentiation of product,* comes in. What makes the product you're selling stand out? Why is it better than every other product being pitched to this investor?

Will your gas stations be the only one in each town? If not, are they going to offer something that no other gas station around offers? Can you sell the gas cheaper or offer better products in the store? Are you going to have charging stations for EVs or the best ice cream in the region out front? What makes this gas station a worthwhile investment compared to all the other options on the investor's table?

Track record and differentiation combine to become a powerful force for demand, trust, and attention—but only if you can sell them. That's why both of these elements are undercut by the third factor in the formula, the *complexity of the story* you can tell about them.

Investors are busy people who are easily distracted, so you need a simple, memorable story that explains why they should keep listening. The simpler your story—that is, how easy it is to grasp, buy into, and *re-explain later*—the more attractive it is.

And that's true whether the story perfectly reflects reality or not. There's a scene in the show *Mad Men* that encapsulates how powerful a simple story is. When trying to rebrand the cigarette company Lucky Strike, the brilliant, troubled ad man Don Draper comes up with the line "It's toasted" to describe how Lucky Strike is different from all the other cigarettes on the market.[11] The fact that this wasn't a distinctive quality about those cigarettes didn't matter. The story was so simple that it made smokers interested in trying a Lucky Strike to see the "toasted" difference.

The opposite is true as well. A line often attributed to Ronald Reagan sums this up nicely: "If you're explaining, you're losing." Even if you have the longest track record and a truly different, highly innovative product, no one will ever know that fact if you struggle to pull those points together in a pithy story. People don't trust complexity. They have no patience for it.

To see the power of a good pitch, consider our story from the last chapter. David's pitch to convince King Saul to give him a shot at Goliath was a perfect example of a short story improving on a limited track record. Roughly, it reads: "I, your servant David, have killed both the lion and the bear. This uncircumcised Philistine, Goliath, will be like one of them, because he has defied the armies of the living God" (see 1 Samuel 17:36).

Nice and simple. I've killed a lion; how much harder can it be to defeat Goliath if I have God on my side?

Any extra complexity would only have hurt David's cause. If he wasted time explaining the nuances of his experience and why he hadn't yet joined the army and why his experience as a shepherd fighting off wolves was so much better than being a soldier . . . Saul would have been far less likely to buy in. But a boy who can kill lions can also kill giants? That's something he could believe.

This is why track record and differentiation are *divided by* the complexity of the story in the Law of Differentiation formula. The more complex it is, the less value both of those elements have in your effort to convince the investor. The simpler the story, the more potent both elements are in persuading your audience.

There's an old saying that in sales, you have three bullets you can fire: the first for explaining what you do, the second for explaining what's in it for the client, and if you need the third bullet to explain anything else, you might as well use it on yourself.

The Law of Trade-Offs

> ### Size x Speed x Terms =
> ### Base Fundraising Potential

The previous chapter explained how to fill a fund: You simply multiply the pipeline, conversion rate, and bite size. However, there are other trade-offs to consider when quantifying the true potential of your fundraising efforts. Of course, all formulas involve an innate sense of trade-off. In physics, Newton's second law states that force equals mass times acceleration, or F=ma. To create more force, you need either more mass, more acceleration, or both. In other words, if you are short on mass or acceleration, you need more of the other to reach the level of force you're looking for.

The Law of Trade-Offs is unique in that it's a formula that requires balancing size, speed, and terms. You can't max out all three variables at once. The other two have to compensate for the one you prioritize. Otherwise, you will miss your base fundraising potential.

Let's put that in real-world terms:

- If you want a large fund or investment (*size*), you can increase the likelihood of success by making it more affordable (*terms*) or being willing to take a longer time frame (*speed*).
- If you need the funds quickly (*speed*), you need to decrease the amount you want to get (*size*) or offer the investor an excellent deal (*terms*).
- If you want to drive a premium on the deal you're selling (*terms*), you likely can't attract a large sum of money (*size*), and you also probably need more time (*speed*).

Whatever you do, you have to balance this equation. If you want to raise $300 million right now (*size*), but you can't make it cheap (*speed*) or offer optimal conditions for investment (*terms*), that's an equation that equals failure.

The Law of Leverage

Differentiation x Sales Resources = Leveraged Fundraising Potential

There are certain things within the fundraiser's power and other things that are not. It is within your power to build and maintain relationships, and strong relationships with investors increase your potential for raising funds for anything.

But there are still limitations. A fundraiser can only leverage what exists. If excellence does not exist within a product—if there is limited potential for significant profit for the investor—the fundraiser cannot create it. They can tell a better story about it, but a great story will still eventually run into the hard truths of reality.

Ideas have intrinsic value. Fundraisers amplify that value through our ability to generate attention—to persuade others to trust us. But we can't make investors demand what has limited value to them. When a fundraiser breaks this law and tries to leverage trust to sell a bad product, it may work temporarily, but longer term, it only hurts the product and the fundraiser.

This is true of every type of marketing. Good marketing amplifies what exists—the qualities that make a product worth purchasing. Combine good marketing with a good product, and you can achieve the *actual full potential for sales*. But good marketing (or fundraising) with a bad product only exposes the weakness of that product. As advertising wizard Jerry Della Femina once told me, "The only thing great marketing does for a bad product is put that product out of business faster."

Jennifer Zimmerman, a colleague of mine I met at General Catalyst, came up with one of the best slogans of the last several decades. She was the mind behind "Come see the softer side of Sears." It was a brilliant marketing campaign (*differentiation*) that drove people to Sears not for the furniture and appliances the company was famous for, but for clothing and similar items customers normally bought at Target or Walmart. Yet after briefly improving sales and revenue, that growth in interest eventually helped put Sears out of business—because people discovered there wasn't a "softer side" to the company. Sears couldn't compete in that area (soft goods), and that made people question whether the furniture and appliance side of the company was equally unimpressive.

Zimmerman had come up with an off-the-charts slogan for differentiation, but Sears lacked the *sales resources* (i.e., the product offerings) to capitalize. In fact, the company's sales resources were so poor, it was essentially like multiplying that perfect differentiation number by a negative. Instead of leveraging what Sears did well, the campaign painted the whole company as an underperformer. That was not the kind of differentiation they were looking for.

Fundraisers, like marketers, aren't magicians. And like marketers, their relationships can be damaged if the potential they promise does not equal the actual potential of the fund. They can't make something true that isn't. You have to sell what you have, not what you wish you had. To do otherwise can only damage the trust investors place in you.

The Law of Money in Motion

Fundraising = Effort x Availability

An object in motion tends to stay in motion. An object at rest tends to stay at rest. This comes from Newton's first law of motion. In fundraising, the easiest investment to source comes from investors with money available that is "in motion" and heading in the same direction as your ideas. The more that available money is heading in your direction (*increasing availability*), the easier it is to secure it in your fund (*less effort*). The momentum does much of the work.

The opposite also holds true. The more that money is stationary or moving in the opposite direction (*decreasing availability*), the more work is required to turn it your way (*greater effort*).

As of the writing of this book, there's a lot of available money in motion heading toward AI and clean tech. If that's the direction you're going as well, it will require far less effort to gain trust and attention, because the demand is already there. If you're moving in a different direction, though, such as a rideshare company, you'll find money is moving against you. No one sees much value in a new Uber. To change that direction, you'll need some incredible differentiation, a great track record, or a really powerful story—and ideally, all three. You'd need a company that was going to do something radically new in the rideshare industry; otherwise, you won't be able to influence the direction that money is currently heading.

All of this leads to a basic question: Who has "money in motion" for you? Again, money in motion often tends to flow in one direction or another. Children have money in motion for games and sweets. Young adult men often have money in motion for fast cars, beer, and cologne. Young professionals have money in motion for suits.

The brilliance of social media, which made Meta one of the largest companies in the world, was recognizing the direction your money was moving and pairing it with further purchases in that space. With your data at their disposal, Meta knew that if you had just bought a house, your money would now be moving toward curtains, rugs, house plants, towels, and new sheets. Their algorithm would populate your Facebook and Instagram feeds with ads that could channel your money in those directions.

Always consider the Law of Money in Motion when you are qualifying potential investors. You want to fill your pipeline with investors who are not overallocated (with money already settled in one place or another) and who would naturally flow their money in the direction of your product. If you find those investors, persuading them to join you will require much less effort from you and your product.

From Science to Process

I know there's a natural desire to chafe against these principles and laws and to seek some way around them, but they are as inflexible as Newton's laws of motion. The principles must be heeded; the equations all have to balance. Otherwise, you are not going to reach the fund size you were anticipating.

All of these laws and principles are essential and immutable. Again, *they are what they are.* You must acknowledge the reality of your circumstances and adapt to them to meet your needs. That's how you win the battle before it ever starts.

This is the science of fundraising, but it is not the whole of fundraising. There is much more to the Tao than the equations that undergird the process. Significantly, none of the principles and laws tell you anything about *how* to win trust or *how* to convince an investor that they truly need what you're selling.

For that, we have to look elsewhere, starting with the processes innate to selling.

Chapter 4

The Fundraising Process

Most people stepping into the fundraising arena think the hardest part is simply getting into the room. That is undeniably a major challenge but it's a mistake to assume the process gets easier once you're finally sitting across from a potential investor.

It doesn't.

The novice fundraiser assumes people *want* to say yes. The sale is almost a secondary concern. As long as the product they are selling appears likely to offer a return, they think investors will leap at the opportunity to throw their money behind it.

This is not the case. In fact, the experienced fundraiser knows that once you get that all-important meeting, you discover that the sale is a complex process that requires a nuanced understanding of the investor's psychology (which we will cover in detail in part 2) as well as an understanding

75

of the nature of the sale itself and the type of organization to which the investor belongs.

The Hard Truths of Fundraising

There are some hard truths that you must accept about the fundraising world if you are going to succeed within it. When you enter the room, the risks are high—almost as high as the rewards—and it takes a certain temperament and a deep commitment to the Tao to take on those risks.

I get perhaps ten calls a day asking if I can introduce some fundraiser to some investor to help them raise money. I almost always say no, not because I'm a jerk but because an introduction won't help. It just never works. Early in my career, I probably introduced hundreds of people to very powerful investors, but nothing ever happened because they lacked the skills to actually make the sale.

Up to this point, I've given you an overview of what fundraising is and why it's valuable. This is the intellectual background that's necessary to be a successful fundraiser. But like an untrained martial arts fighter who has read a few books about jiu jitsu or karate, intellect alone won't really lead you to victory. Fundraising and fighting aren't just about book smarts; they're about training and developing key skills to enable you to win. So, from here on, I'm going to lay out the skills you need to actually enter and fight in the arena—and to win once you get there.

Understanding the People

The process starts by recognizing who is going to be in the room with you. The vast majority of those who control and manage resources in our country are white and male. It should not be a surprise, then, that they often make up the majority of people in the room. A victory for them, almost by definition, strengthens the hierarchies already deeply entrenched in our society. They are the ones who will most benefit from your efforts.

To a certain degree, it could not be any other way. The people who are already in the room must have more access to capital than anyone else. To have more access to capital, they must come from or represent the strongest forces within our financial system. To be successful in this field, you will have to speak to them in a way they want to be spoken to, and you will be required to find ways to increase the size of their bank account—even if they are the ones who need it least.

This is simply the nature of modern American capitalism. *It is what it is.*

That doesn't mean this is the only group to benefit. There is considerable potential to enrich all those involved in this practice. The wealth of the billionaire class can grow while also providing opportunities, riches, and support for members of many other communities. But wealthy investors will almost always also be rewarded along the way.

You may be completely indifferent to this point, or you may have a strong reaction against it. Like it or not, you have no choice but to make peace with this reality if you want to realize your own ambitions.

Not only that, but once again, you'll have to adapt to the type of organization those with the resources have put in place to manage those resources. However they organize the business structures around them, you have to understand the investment on their terms and approach it from their perspective.

Understanding the System

When you talk to someone in the room, it isn't always about what you are offering them or how much you want them to invest. Often, it's a matter of how you fit into their system.

Resources—provided they are valuable enough—always require organizations to manage them. These organizations typically fall into three main categories:

1. **Tribal System:** When a group shares their resources and attempts to distribute them "fairly" throughout the organization.

2. **Monarchic System:** When an organization develops around an individual or a family who controls the resources and centralizes decision-making.

3. **Meritocratic System:** When a community shares the resources by appointing and dismissing leaders to manage those resources.

What makes a resource valuable? Scarcity. People will always organize around scarcity. It's hardwired into our

DNA to do whatever we can to avoid it, and nothing reduces our fear of scarcity as much as owning or managing those resources ourselves. The money you seek for investment is scarce, just as oil, diamonds, platinum, water, or food are scarce.

The rooms you're trying to enter as a fundraiser will all protect and expand their resources by organizing into one of these three systems, and failing to understand and adapt to the right system is one of the most significant pitfalls you could fall into.

These three systems aren't entirely unique to fundraising. They are also popular configurations for governments, which are really just large political entities designed to protect and distribute resources. Since systems are so important to fundraising, it's worth digging into them a bit deeper—including how your efforts should fit into those systems.

Tribal Systems

The tribal system involves a group of decision-makers who share their resources (i.e., money) and collectively bear the risks and reap the gains of those resources. Here, investment decisions are made together. This is something like a political confederacy: an association between various autonomous groups or individuals. Tribes band together for their shared interest, just as countries join organizations like NATO or the European Union to strengthen defense or promote their GDP.

In fundraising, you often find tribal confederations organized in "investment clubs" (in which you, me, and four or five others decide to invest together) and in groups of investors focused on similar interests or specializations. For instance, you might find several individuals working together to produce films or theater productions. There are also tribal confederations that invest solely in restaurants and angel investors focused on technology in Silicon Valley, for example.

The key to working within this system is to recognize the power of persuasion and consensus within these groups. Because there is no single "decider" in this system, fundraisers have to persuade the entire tribe—either one or two at a time or all at once.

If you meet with individuals within the tribe, your aim should be not just to persuade them but to either earn access to other members of the tribe or to give them the tools to build consensus within the tribe themselves. We'll discuss how to do this more in the next part of the book.

For now, let's focus on your aim, which is to get the idea behind your fund to go viral within this community.

So, if you're walking into a tribal room, you have to ask yourself a few questions: Are enough members of the tribe there to make a decision? If not, do you have a path to meet with more? Do you have the means to get the members you've met to build consensus for you?

Monarchical Systems

We all know how monarchies work. The king or queen owns the resources, and everyone organizes around that. Sometimes, some of the leader's relatives have access to some of the resources. Everyone else is there to protect the monarch and their resources. We've already examined this approach under another name: the feudal system. We found that feudal Japan had nobles with access to the royal family, samurai/knights who protected access to nobles and royalty, and peasants who worked to build resources but who had no control over them.

Monarchical systems, or *kingdoms*, share many similarities with autocratic political systems and can be very durable. They only fall apart when resources are lost or when they're taken over by a hostile force. In other words, unless the vault is empty or there's been a coup, the system remains intact.

In fundraising, these "monarchs" are usually wealthy individuals or families and, just as in a ruling monarchy, the wealth is usually concentrated in a few family hands and passed down through the generations. Each generation invests to build the wealth for the next. A similar system is also in place for managing the sovereign funds of many monarchic countries, such as those found in the Middle East.

One final version of this system in fundraising sometimes exists in companies built by one person. That person may, in theory, be replaceable, as they would be in the meritocratic corporate structure we'll cover in a moment.

However, some corporations have CEOs who could never *really* be replaced or who could only be removed through some kind of coup or revolution. Consider Elon Musk at Tesla. Technically, the board could remove him, but he is so deeply entwined with Tesla that such a change is hard to fathom. And the Tesla that emerged from that process would be an entirely different entity than it is today.

In other words, Tesla is Musk's personal kingdom, whether people like it or not.

There are no particular rules to follow for the king, as there are in democracies. If the person at the top likes what you say, you get the investment. If they don't, you don't.

For that reason, your aim has to be to climb the hierarchy until you can either get to the king or to someone who can convince the king for you—a noble or someone in the royal family.

There are certain questions you have to ask yourself when pitching your fund to a monarchy: Are you talking to a nobleman, a relative of the monarch, or the monarch himself/herself? If not, what is this person's rank in the hierarchy? If they are a peasant, can they get you in front of a samurai/knight? If it's a guardian of some sort, can they get you to a noble? Can the noble get you in front of the king?

The entire process is about gaining access to increasingly exclusive rooms.

Meritocratic Systems

In the meritocratic (or *corporate*) system, we find the sort of organizations most people outside the fundraising world think of when we talk about fundraising. This category includes the large investment banks like JPMorgan and Goldman Sachs. The power to control resources in these institutions is determined by some attempt at a meritocratic process. In its ideal form, a CEO is elected by the board based on their skill and record of success. They are responsible to the board and shareholders. And they—like everyone else in the organization—can be fired and replaced if they fail to live up to the standards set for their position.

It's important to note that most corporate systems *claim* to be meritocratic but aren't really based on merit at all. They pay lip service to merit, but, in the end, they are primarily political systems resembling kingdoms or tribes. The key distinction is how long the leader is entitled to keep their job. In a corporation, those granted power only get a certain amount of time to produce the results that the people who placed them in the position desire. If they don't do their job well, they can be kicked out.

For the fundraiser, there's another, more important, distinctive quality of corporate systems: They have a unique set of rules—or a "constitution"—that governs their decision-making process. For instance, even if you live in a country that claims to be meritocratic—as most democracies do—you know how much of life is governed by the local laws and bureaucracy in place. This isn't true for a monarchy that can change a law on a whim. And tribes rely far more on customs and traditions to make decisions.

By contrast, investors working in corporate institutions exercise power through existing rules rather than by creating new ones. To win their investment, then, you have to tailor your approach to the rules already in place. For example, if an investment firm has rules that require it to focus on low-risk investments in US-based technology and retail companies, your high-risk medical company based in Switzerland won't see a dime of their money. Occasionally, there may be some room to persuade members of a corporation to bend one rule or another, but you can't come in with a project that fails to fit the general parameters of the company.

If you're trying to appeal to a corporate meritocratic system, then, you have a different set of questions to answer: Do you know the rules? Do you know the boxes they need to check? Does your investment or fund fit those parameters? Do you have a way around any of the rules you don't fit?

Remember, in a corporation, you aren't selling to people; you're proving you fit their rules. That's the name of the game.

The Battle for Attention

Understanding and working within a system is a great start to improving your fund's odds of success, but, unfortunately, it's only the start of the actual selling process. Just because you are in the right room and know what's required doesn't mean you can actually make a sale. That requires powerful tools of persuasion (which is the entire focus of the second part of this book), as well as an understanding of the *battle for attention* within the sales process.

In the battle for attention, selling can seem simple in its basic premise: You make the pitch, you re-qualify, and you land the sale. But to actually do that requires mastering many different processes and concepts.

This is the art of gaining and keeping attention long enough to close the sale. No matter what system you are working within as a fundraiser, it is only by maintaining full attention that you can establish a connection, share your ideas effectively, and convince someone to hand over their money to you. The value of attention can't be overemphasized in this field.

In my own quest to hold attention as a fundraiser, I have developed multiple speaking techniques. As a rule, I speak in quick, stochastic bursts and vary my volume for emphasis to keep people focused on what I'm saying. I gesticulate to catch the eye of everyone else in the room. I signpost my conversation with phrases like "This is the last point I'm going to make on this topic" to hold on to their precious attention just a little longer before finally releasing it. In every sale, it's a constant battle between attention and distraction, and I do whatever I can to tip the odds in my favor.

The most successful politicians—from Bill Clinton to Barack Obama to Donald Trump—are masters of this, as are the great entertainers like Jerry Seinfeld and Chris Rock. They have their unique styles, but they all know how to gather attention from a crowd and hold it for long periods.

Charisma helps in this effort, but prioritizing charisma is misleading. Charisma offers an enticing shortcut to the sale. It's like Goliath entering the fight. But like Goliath's size and strength, charisma can take you only so far—and it often creates blind spots. Goliaths of charisma may assume their charm will get them to yes without any further effort, and sometimes it does. But charm is rooted in the goal of "I want you to want me." A charismatic individual can often turn off potential investors because they are perceived as too slick or self-absorbed. A David who develops mastery of controlling attention with grace and calm can often achieve much greater results.

To develop such mastery, we have to turn to a well-established process in sales: the *sales call*. This term doesn't necessarily require a "call" as it did in the days when sales-people got on the phone to sell you their products. These days, it simply refers to holding a meeting for the purpose of hearing a sales pitch.

At first, applying this process may require conscious effort—marking out each stage of the conversation and consciously seeking the right comment to move it forward. With practice, though, it becomes second nature and unconscious. Regardless of how naturally the sales call comes to you, practice is absolutely crucial. I am reminded of an expression apocryphally attributed to the ancient Greek poet Archilochus: In stressful situations, we don't rise to the level of our expectations; we fall to the level of our training.

That said, the pathway to successful pitching and maintaining attention follows a set formula:

1. Gain Attention
2. Establish Rapport
3. Generate Interest
4. Establish Credibility

5. Discuss Needs and Qualify
6. Present Solutions and Qualify
7. Close

The first four steps don't have to happen in order, but they should all happen. For clarity's sake, though, I'll explain them in the order presented above.

First, you need to *gain someone's attention*. You can gain it through something you say, something you do, or something you wear—anything that helps get the person to shift their focus onto you.

Second, in one way or another, you need to *establish rapport* by creating a sense of connection. Essentially, you need to find a way to communicate, "I like you. I'm like you. I am interested in you. I want you to be interested in me."

This may come in the form of a humorous comment or an interesting fact that draws them into the conversation. The ability to effortlessly establish rapport is why engaging and attractive people have so much success in sales. Others naturally want to get closer to such people. However you do it, rapport helps your conversation partner pay further attention by setting aside whatever thoughts were in their mind before it began.

Third, *generating interest* should turn your audience toward what you're selling. A common technique is to say something special about your product, service, or proposition. It should be short and sweet to get them to respond, "I want to hear more." Quite literally, most marketing professionals and journalists employ this technique in advertising and writing for every single ad or article. I would argue that the success of many social media platforms is rooted in their addictive ways of generating interest that keep you buying in over and over again.

Fourth, at some point in these early moments of conversation, you must *establish credibility* by showing you're someone they can trust. You need to prove that you have the right to pitch the investor.

Once you have set the stage and the investor has been primed, only then do you want to start selling. That occurs in the fifth step, *discussing their needs*. This has to occur so late in the process because you must first understand what they're looking to gain out of a potential investment. If you try to find this out too soon, they will not pay attention. However, if you have gone through the appropriate sales call setup, then you are ready to ask the *magic question*: "If I could show you how to solve your problem or make you money, would you be interested?"

If they qualify themselves (i.e., they either say yes or tell you under what conditions they *would* say yes), now's the time for you to move on to step six, *presenting your solution*. This is your pitch. Your pitch should solve the problem they've already introduced. If it does, and you've established enough trust and interest while maintaining attention, then you can close the deal.

This is the process behind every interaction that leads to some sort of transaction. Among other contexts, you see it in the most stereotypical sale of all: cars.

A car dealership puts their shiniest, nicest vehicles out front. Or perhaps they put out a sign that advertises a special deal. They know that almost every customer wants one of those vehicles or wants a deal, and presenting their best models or special discount opportunity before you even walk in generates interest immediately. Once you're in the showroom, the salesperson will come up and chat with you a bit—establishing rapport. They don't leap into the sale; instead, they engage in small talk. They might ask you about your day or your family. They might mention the weather or how busy the lot has been lately. They then build credibility by telling you about a car's reliability rating and fancy warranty they offer. They tell you they can offer such a good deal because you've come in at the end of the month when there's more leverage to cut prices. They appear to be letting you in on trade secrets—showing you that they think you're special and they're a different kind of salesperson.

At this point, they haven't pushed for a sale at all, but they have earned your attention and a sense that they know what they're doing and they're on your side.

Then, they start asking about your needs and qualifying them. "I saw you looking at that beautiful red sports car out front. Do you want to test drive it?" When you tell them you're looking for a minivan, they pivot to that pitch—talking about the safety features and the great mileage. They explain how it's the best vehicle to address your specific needs. If you continue to qualify yourself and show your interest, they start talking numbers. "I know the sticker says $32,500, but let me talk to my manager. I think we could get that down to an even $30,000 for you." At this point, they have your attention, they have your trust, and soon, they have your yes. They close the deal, and you buy the minivan.

The sales call process doesn't have to involve an exchange of cash. We use it when we flirt with someone at a bar. We dress in a way that creates general interest, wearing nice clothes, expensive cologne or perfume, and a nice watch or our best makeup. When we see someone we find attractive, we engage in small talk to build rapport and generate further interest by trying to be charming or funny or sexy. We establish credibility by suggesting we aren't like the other people in the bar. We're funnier, or more thoughtful, or more genuine. There's something about us that's different. We tell them that they can trust us, that this isn't a lascivious pickup game. Or perhaps this is just a bit of fun, and they won't have to worry about us bothering them again.

With trust and credibility in place, we ask what they like and what they're interested in. If we hear they love a certain musician, we might suggest a solution—"There's a place just around the corner that plays music I think you'll enjoy. Do you want to go check it out?" If we're on the same page, we head off together on our first date.

As a caution to the readers of this book, there is a way to do this in a manipulative fashion—such as how pickup artists take advantage of this sort of interaction to undermine a person's confidence and trick them into an intimate experience, or how a huckster salesman can manipulate you into buying a car you don't actually want—but at root, this process happens innately and naturally. It's simply how we as humans suggest what we want, see if the other person is interested, and make any sort of agreement. This is a key component for how humans connect, organize, and find solutions.

I use this same formula in every pitch I make. I might use it a dozen times today. This is the template. You just have to fill in the blanks.

Sales and Human Nature

Here's the bad news: There are no shortcuts to these processes. You have to follow each step. Just like the inflexible laws and principles in the previous two chapters, you can't cheat your way to yes in the sale. You can't charisma your way around the systems in place. But the reason behind that is good news: This is simply how humans behave—and understanding that provides immense potential opportunity across your life.

By understanding the systems protecting resources, you can know exactly what is required of you to get to the yes that unlocks funds. With the sales call process, you can walk into any conversation and know where you are at any time.

Like everything else in the Tao, we are just tracking *what is*. Greater understanding of *what is* generates greater potential to realize your desires across your entire life. Ignoring these natural processes just leaves value on the table.

But to really maximize your ability to secure funding— or anything else in life—we have to go deeper into human nature. Lurking under the surface of all the guidance in this chapter is a concept that is central to fundraising success: *persuasion*. In every system and every sale, someone somewhere has to be persuaded to hand money over to you.

Success at persuasion requires more than the tools we've covered so far. You need to understand the human psychology behind how human beings get to yes and why they are driven to say no. And to do that, you'll need to start with the Tao's theory of mind.

PART TWO

The Art of Persuasion

Chapter 5

A Theory of Mind

When my mother died in 2023, it was, as you can imagine, a deeply upsetting time for me. But the mind is a funny thing. In that period of grief, my mind wasn't content to simply dwell on that singular sad event. It sought out more sadness.

In that first month after her passing, I remember sitting in a hotel room in Austin, Texas, and instead of focusing on recollections of my mother or the many responsibilities I had to fulfill that day, my mind kept coming up with unrelated stories that riffed on the theme of my underlying sadness. It unearthed memories I hadn't thought of for years. I pictured everything from my dog, Daisy, who had died five years earlier, to moments when I was bullied as a child in Minnesota.

The sadness I felt that day was not about those past events, but my mind got confused. It misplaced the source of my sadness and brought other potential candidates to the surface. It started telling me the wrong story to explain why I felt the way I did.

In other words, my mind was playing a trick on me. The human brain is a remarkable machine, but it isn't perfect. It works in an ad hoc fashion based on how it evolved. In certain situations, the wires tend to get crossed.

This isn't just an interesting phenomenon for the fundraiser. It's essential knowledge. If we want to raise funds, we have to learn to persuade others. And if we want to persuade others, we have to first understand how the brain processes the arguments we're making. But before we can do that, we'll need a theory of mind.

The Tao's Understanding of the Mind

At the outset of our overview of the Tao's theory of mind, it's important to discuss two points up front: first, why persuasion is so important to fundraising, and second, what I mean by "theory of mind" in this context.

There's only so much you can do as a fundraiser by understanding the processes involved. Once you get into the right room, know the type of room you're in, and know the process to get someone to yes, you still have to do the hardest job of all: persuade them to agree with you. Persuasion is the oil that greases all the steps of the sales process. It's what allows you to generate interest; it's why you need to establish rapport; it's what takes you from discussing needs to presenting a solution; and it's the only road to a successful close.

Simply put, without persuasion, nothing happens in the room.

To persuade anyone regularly and effectively, you need a system—and a system anchored in a theory of mind is always best. Psychologists use the term "theory of mind" to refer to our ability to think about the mental state of others, even though we lack direct access to their minds. It includes how well we understand their emotional state and needs.

Theory of mind in this book is related, but different. You might consider it a *theory of* theory of mind—or rather, a theory of *how* the other person in the room is thinking. The main focus will be on examining how we can best address the emotional and psychological needs of the investor as they go through the process of getting to yes.

There are many approaches to explain the inner workings of our thoughts—and this book is agnostic on whether the Tao's is the best or most accurate. What is important here is that the Tao's theory of mind accurately relates how others think and react in the fundraising environment. In reality, all theories are incomplete, but some are more useful than others. And the Tao's theory of mind should be helpful in the types of interactions we have when fundraising.

An "Other-Focused" Practice

Definitions out of the way, the most unique element of the Tao is its theory of mind focus. Unlike other philosophies, the perspective of the Tao is not attuned to *you* and how *you* think but toward *the other person* in the room and *their* thoughts.

This requires a shift in our natural perspective. To accomplish this shift, we must take inspiration from Nicolaus Copernicus, who is most famous for developing the theory of heliocentrism—a model that placed the Sun at the center of the universe instead of the Earth. He was wrong on the details (the Sun isn't the center of the whole universe, after all), but his overall framework was correct—and it's the correct framework for approaching persuasion as well.

By definition, in fundraising, there's always another person involved. And if you want to persuade them, you have to prioritize their experience of this encounter. The person with the money is your sun, and *you* must revolve around *them*. You have to consider their perspective, their needs, and their attention in everything.

The first order of business in adjusting this perspective is recognizing that *you* are not the center of *their* universe. When you meet an investor, you should always assume that the moment before they met you, they were thinking about something else entirely. They were thinking about another pitch, the fact that their tooth aches, or the need to clear space on their schedule to see their kid's school performance. This is the most important moment in your day, but it isn't in theirs. They're thinking about their life, not your objectives or needs.

In your efforts to gain their attention, earn their trust, stoke their interest, and ultimately create a fundraising atomic reaction, you must always place their experience of this interaction at the center of your efforts.

If I walk into a meeting with an investor and think only about myself, my focus remains firmly on what I want. But this introduces blind spots into the interaction. I approach the conversation through *my* needs and use the arguments that *I* find appealing. I miss the cues that could tell me what the other person in the room is thinking and feeling—consciously and subconsciously. And that means I leave their concerns unaddressed.

Remember, *the default answer for every investor is no.* They say no far more than they say yes. If you want to change their mind, you have to understand what is on their mind and speak to those core needs.

This is where the theory of mind comes in. The Tao's theory of mind breaks down what the investor wants, what they fear, and the natural direction their thoughts turn when they experience a problem. To persuade them through your pitch, to address their objections, and to close the deal, you have to counter all the impulses in their mind that are drawing them toward no.

This is how you do it.

How the Brain Works

The Tao's theory of mind is founded on an understanding of how the brain works. This is obviously not going to be an exhaustive treatment. I'm putting immense amounts of science and medicine to one side. But in this simple outline, there's much truth that can help us understand what the other person in the room is thinking.

What we consider thinking is really the collaborative effort of three competing components of our brain: the *hindbrain*; the *frontal lobe*; and the *ego* that is our sense of self, our consciousness. The hindbrain is what sometimes gets referred to as the "reptile brain." This is the part that every animal has. It's purely reactive and hardwired for survival. This is where our instincts come from. The hindbrain tells us to run when we see a volcano erupting or to fight when we're caught in an alley and someone is coming toward us. This is the part of the brain that tells parents to put their child before themselves. It's where an animal gets its sense of how to hunt from the moment it's born.

Central to this part of our brain are our emotions, which are often connected directly to stimuli we experience. Someone shouts at us, and we feel hurt or scared or angry. We meet someone important, and we feel nervous. Someone we care about dies, and we feel sadness.

This is the type of intelligence we can easily observe in our pets. You come home, and your dog is happy. You snap at the dog for taking food off the table, and they feel shame. Their emotions are immediate and connect to what is happening in front of them at that moment. Every dog owner knows there's no point in punishing a dog for something they did hours before. The dog's brain can't associate the act with the punishment.

The human brain has evolved beyond that animal hindbrain. We also possess a frontal lobe. This is our logical, interpreting, timekeeping part of the brain. It's where all our "thinking" takes place. It's also our creative engine. It's the problem solver and the storyteller. We love the frontal lobe because it's what separates us not just from other modern animals but from the other ancient hominids. While it's currently disputed in the latest science, it has been said that humanity became the dominant species because we could outthink our direct competitors. Our logic and creative skills were more advanced. The frontal lobe allowed us to create tools, strategies, reciprocity, and community—making us greater than the sum of our individual parts.

Other animals have some elements of this thinking capacity. Dogs understand reciprocity and community on some basic level—as do elephants, dolphins, and whales, to name a few. Chimpanzees and some birds use rudimentary tools. But nobody thinks like us.

These two parts of the brain are in constant conversation, in what scientists call a *cognitive emotional loop*. When a stimulus enters the brain, the hindbrain might get scared. At that point, the frontal lobe asks, "What am I scared of?" And it comes up with a story to explain the emotion. From that story, we develop a solution.

This is a powerful survival technique. The hindbrain may experience that fear looking at a forest. The frontal lobe remembers that a tiger recently attacked someone in that forest. Connecting the emotion to the story not only keeps us from entering the forest on instinct but also allows us to develop a strategy to catch the tiger or to find a better path to our destination.

This conversation can also work the other way. The frontal lobe can remember that we have a huge meeting early on Wednesday. That then inspires the hindbrain to feel anxiety. Associating our connection to time and memory with emotion can allow us to learn and prepare.

It's a remarkable system—but there's one problem: The frontal lobe and the hindbrain aren't always completely on the same page about the cause of these emotions or the proper response to them. There isn't always a one-to-one connection between what we feel and the story the frontal lobe tells us about that emotion. This is why my sense of sadness at my mother's passing could also make me think about a dog of mine who died many years ago.

This mix-up—called *transference* in psychology—occurs all the time. We come home stressed out from a long day in the office when things weren't going well. At dinner, our kid spills his soup, and we yell at him because the frontal lobe has projected the frustration from work onto the wrong target.

This is all complicated enough, but there's another component in your head: *you*. This is your ego, the part of your mind that exists to give you a harmonized personality that integrates the stories and memories of the frontal lobe with the emotions and instincts of the hindbrain. The ego is responsible for creating our sense of individuality. It's what gives us a unique perspective.

You can think of the ego as your operating system. It sorts through the stimuli we experience and the various impulses we have coming from the hindbrain and frontal lobe. It also tells us who we are and creates a continuous story for how we are moving through the universe.

The ego has one other crucially important aspect. It generates our desires and our sense of self-belief. These desires can lead humans to immense achievement. If Tom Brady didn't have an ego that intensely craved winning, he wouldn't have won seven Super Bowls and, arguably, become the greatest quarterback of all time. If Edison didn't have an ego that believed he could change the world, he never would have invented the incandescent light bulb.

But that same capacity for desire can make the ego a bottomless pit of need. Whatever we feed it, it wants more of that. It will chase after desire unendingly. Uncontrolled, it can destroy deeper needs to reach whatever it is seeking. The ego wants sex with beautiful people, even if that will destroy your marriage and your relationship with your children. It wants rich food, even if indulging harms your health. It wants wealth, even if amassing money means compromising your most sacred ethics and values. We all wrestle with satisfying and taming the ego to get through life.

Speaking to the Whole Mind

All of this may feel very off-topic for a book about fundraising and achieving investment, but understanding how the brain works is central to persuading investors. Our job is to get the investor to say yes. Many novice fundraisers approach this through logic, targeting the frontal lobe. But just focusing on the frontal lobe ignores the other players in the investor's head—the hindbrain that exists in the world of emotion and the ego that is focused on its desires.

If you can address all three parties, though, you can create an incredibly compelling argument in your favor. In fact, you can even overwhelm the logic centers of the frontal lobe.

In 1995, O. J. Simpson was on trial for the murder of his ex-wife, Nicole Brown, and her friend Ron Goldman. There's overwhelming consensus that O. J. did it. The evidence has always pointed to him. Yet, largely thanks to the work of his lead defense attorney, Johnnie Cochran, he was exonerated.

Cochran was a master persuader. He knew the jury had a logical sense that O. J. had done it. Still, there was an emotional pull from the hindbrain that made them reticent to convict. O. J. was very likable. He was handsome and funny. He'd been a star athlete and a successful actor. People loved him. To get to "not guilty," though, the minds of the jury needed a story they could tell themselves to explain their decision—a story they could also use to justify their decision to others. Their egos desired respect from their families and peers. It didn't want to be scared of explaining their decision.

So, Cochran gave the jury the story they needed, a story that aligned with the hindbrain's emotional preference and the ego's desire to avoid the fear of expressing the wrong thing.

Before dropping his masterpiece slogan, he created ethical space for the jury by clarifying their role. He got Judge Lance Ito to agree that the jury's role wasn't to determine guilt but to adjudicate the law. And the law said that their job was to weigh whether O. J.'s actions were beyond any *reasonable doubt.* At this point, there was a little daylight between the logical conclusion of the evidence and the emotional preference in the jury. Then, he used the law of differentiation to transform the immense complexity of the case into a story as simple as possible. You've probably heard that story before: "If [the glove] doesn't fit, you must acquit."[12]

That was enough. With that line, Cochran won O. J.'s freedom, despite all the logic working against him.

I don't want to pass over too quickly the power of this lesson. When you understand the Tao's theory of mind and place your audience at the center of your universe, a well-delivered line can change everything.

The most useful lesson anyone can learn about fundraising is to give their audience a phrase they can repeat to others to explain why a decision was made. If you can simplify your pitch to a single phrase that people can repeat, that means two things: first, you used Occam's Razor to get to the core of the story, and second, you helped people find an acceptable reason why they made a decision. And that acceptance harmonizes the competing parts of their brains. If they emotionally wanted to get there but needed a scrap of logic to take them, this story will do it.

It's the reason everyone, from presidents to massive corporations, seeks out slogans.

"Built Ford tough."

"Guns don't kill people, people kill people."

"No child left behind."

"Nobody ever got fired for buying IBM."

"Make love, not war."

"The Happiest Place on Earth."

"Ask not what your country can do for you, ask what you can do for your country."

We did this at my former company, General Catalyst, where we told our clients that we are "investing in powerful, positive change that endures." Who doesn't want to be part of that? It's emotionally exciting. It's logically compelling. It's succinct.

This is the power of the brevity of your story.

This same potential is available to any fundraiser using the Tao's theory of mind. When we place the investor as our sun and focus on the internal battle within the various aspects of their mind, we can service each part of their brain, providing whatever they need to win the argument and agree to the investment.

Chapter 6

Stoking Desire

The art of persuasion goes as far back as literature, rhetoric, and deep thought. To show you this, I ask you to indulge me in a short literary analysis of arguably the greatest writer of all time, William Shakespeare. His play *Julius Caesar* pivots in act 3. Up until that point, Caesar is the play's main character and its focus. But then, in the first scene of that third act, Shakespeare depicts the most famous assassination in history, and Caesar—our focal character—dies, leaving us to wonder who our new hero will be.

At the beginning of scene 2, it appears that our new hero is Brutus, Caesar's former friend and one of his chief assassins. At Caesar's funeral, Brutus speaks first and successfully convinces the Roman people by arguing very logically that Caesar had to go:

> If then that friend demand
> why Brutus rose against Caesar, this is my answer:
> not that I loved Caesar less, but that I loved
> Rome more. Had you rather Caesar were living, and
> die all slaves, than that Caesar were dead, to live
> all free men?[13]

Just look at the nature of the language here. It's all hypotheticals and logical sentence structure. It makes a compelling, if slightly cold, case for why Brutus killing Caesar was in the public's best interest. But then Marc Antony steps forward to address the crowd.

> Friends, Romans, countrymen, lend me your ears;
> I come to bury Caesar, not to praise him.
> The evil that men do lives after them;
> The good is oft interred with their bones;
> So let it be with Caesar. The noble Brutus
> Hath told you Caesar was ambitious:
> If it were so, it was a grievous fault,
> And grievously hath Caesar answer'd it.[14]

Thus begins one of the most famous pieces of oratory ever written. By the end of the speech, Antony has won over the Roman people, and Brutus—who only a moment before thought he would be treated as a hero—suddenly discovers he's become public enemy number one.

Antony accomplishes this incredible reversal by outdoing Brutus's rhetorical skill, employing the oldest tools of persuasion around: *logos*, *ethos*, and *pathos*—roughly translated to logic, ethics (or values), and emotion, respectively.

Aristotle argued that a great rhetorician should use all three tools to persuade an audience. And Antony does just that in his efforts to persuade his audience that Caesar deserved better—and that the assassins deserved much worse.

Antony, like Brutus, does speak to the logic of the audience in his speech. He lists the good things Caesar has done for Rome, mentioning that Caesar brought captives to Rome whose ransom enriched the city. He also reminds the Romans that Caesar had refused a crown three times, logically arguing that Caesar wasn't after a power grab, as the assassins suggested.

But he doesn't stop there. He also hits on the ethics and values of the audience. He laments that what good people do is often forgotten when they die: "interred with their bones." That just doesn't seem right for someone like Caesar, whom Antony says was a "friend, faithful and just." He argues that because Caesar was so good to Rome, it would only be right for the Romans to mourn him. And he repeatedly uses the word "honorable" ironically when referring to Brutus, with the intention of showing that Caesar was the truly honorable one.

That would be enough for a very convincing speech, but Antony drives the dagger even deeper by adding an emotional layer on top. Look at the emotional words Antony uses in the excerpt above, in particular the word "grievous." He immediately channels the crowd's grief at losing Caesar. He doubles down on that later. "My heart is in the coffin there with Caesar," he says at the end of his speech. "And I must pause until it comes back to me."[15]

Talk about a tearjerker.

Logic, values, and emotion: With those three elements, Antony closes the deal and convinces Rome to change its mind. Fans of the Bard's work know what happens afterward: Brutus and the other assassins flee, and Antony and a young Octavian pursue and defeat them.

So ends the play and the Roman Republic—arguably lost on the quality of one piece of persuasion.

The Persuasion Equation

Persuasion = Desire − Fear

As we've already seen, fundraising can be quite a scientific process, built upon many structures and equations, but ultimately, at its center, it is an act of persuasion. Without persuasion, fundraising is fundamentally impossible. Unless your investment opportunity is an obvious slam dunk, the hindbrain, frontal lobe, and ego are usually in conflict over the decision. The instinct is to say no. To persuade someone to go against this instinct, you have to adjust two variables: *desire* and *fear*, maximizing the former and minimizing the latter. The more successful you are at "dialing in" those two factors, the more likely you are to get to yes.

Desire and fear are always the central variables whenever you try to persuade someone—even yourself—to do anything. You have to *want to do it*, and you have to want to do it more than *you're scared of doing it*. Take skydiving: Your desire to experience the thrill of free-falling and floating safely to earth must be greater than your fear of jumping out of an airplane. If you have an immense fear of heights, it will take an enormous amount of desire to get you strapped into that parachute.

The same is true of starting a family. You may love kids, but if your fear of how parenting will affect your life is greater than your excitement to raise children, you probably won't choose to have them.

Of course, accidents do happen. Sometimes, we opt for impulse purchases or make decisions we later regret. We buy fast food when we're on a diet because, at least momentarily, we want a greasy burger more than we want to fit into those skinny jeans. Some people have affairs because a fleeting sexual impulse outweighs their fear of losing their families and half their income.

In fundraising, though, such impulsive acts are rare. Remember, the other person in the room is the sun. They are in control, and they default to no. They hear offers like yours several times a day, and they wouldn't have gotten into that position if they gave in to momentary desire in the investment space.

To convince them to switch to yes, you have to use the right tools to increase their desire to invest while reducing their fear that it could be the wrong call.

The Nature of Desire

You may have heard of these two components of persuasion before. Usually, though, they are packaged in a different way. It isn't fear and desire; it's fear and *greed*.

I haven't changed this wording to fool you into thinking this idea is original. I have adjusted the language because "greed" is far too limited in its meaning. Greed is a moral term—specifically a *negative* moral term. It suggests indulgence and reaching for what is beyond necessary. The word conjures images of Ebenezer Scrooge and Gordon Gekko.

Undeniably, greed is at play in some investments. People with a great deal of money will invest to ensure they have even more. At times, the returns can feel egregious and beyond all reason.

But the impulse to invest is not limited to greed. Greed is on the spectrum of desires that can influence an investor to say yes. The impulse to accrue millions just for the sake of it is a cousin of the impulse to give away millions to help others. They're simply on opposite ends of the spectrum. We can desire to feed children, end wars, and find cures for cancer as easily as we desire more zeroes added to our bank balance.

This is not only an important moral argument; it's also key to persuading your audience. If you walk into the room assuming an investor's only desire is to indulge in greed, you may miss other important desires—a desire to give back, to lift others up, or to experience the pleasure of seeing their instincts proven correct.

Ancient Rhetoric

Another reason to use desire over greed is that greed fails to describe a central element in our continued evolution. I mentioned in the previous chapter how the ego is our desire engine and that those desires have allowed humans to reach ever-greater heights.

A famous George Mallory quote comes to mind. When asked why he climbed Everest, he answered, "Because it's there."[16] In other words, because a mountain is there, the desire to climb it innately exists—at least in some of us. This same impulse drove us to circumnavigate the globe, go to the moon, and invent all the systems and tools that allow us to live modern lives. Human society simply couldn't exist without this desire.

Buddhists believe in the end of such desire through enlightenment. But crucially, enlightenment involves *exiting* the human experience. Achieving this exit removes us from *Samsara*, the Buddhist view of our current world and the cycle of rebirth. In other words, to remove desire is to stop being human, and to be human is to desire. I applaud and admire anyone who is on that journey. But if you are interested in fundraising, then it's best to consider the power of desire in every human being.

To influence this desire, we need logos, ethos, and pathos. These concepts are so powerful that you will find them far beyond ancient philosophy and early modern literature. Once you know what to look for, you'll find them everywhere.

For instance, we often break our human experience into three categories: heart, mind, and body. But this is only a restatement of logos, ethos, and pathos. The mind is our source of logic. We associate the heart with the center of our emotions. And the body has an intuitive sense of values. We've all felt a physical reaction to things we are deeply for or against, like the rush of passion for a cause we believe is right or a sense of disgust for what we deeply reject.

This same pattern plays out in our popular culture today. Take *Star Trek*. Whether you're a Trekkie like me or not, you've surely heard of the most famous characters who crewed the *Enterprise*: Captain Kirk, Spock, and Bones (i.e., McCoy). They represented a cohesive unit in which their very different personalities all gelled. These personality types worked so well together because they mapped perfectly into logos, ethos, and pathos: Spock was the living embodiment of logos. He was a Vulcan, a thoroughly logical species with very little emotion. Kirk, on the other hand, was all passion and bravado, a real pathos character you could emotionally root for. Bones was the moral compass that looked after the well-being of the crew.

This theory of rhetoric has been in practice for almost twenty-five hundred years, and it's still bearing fruit today by captivating and persuading audiences. Watch any successful political speech, and you'll see the politician hit all three elements—logos, ethos, and pathos—at some point along the way. Tune into any successful marketing campaign, and you'll see how they lean into at least one of these three. The same three categories are central to creating a fundraising atomic reaction.

Creating a Balanced Argument

In order to thoroughly convince somebody of anything, you should incorporate all three of these elements into your pitch—but that doesn't mean the balance should be the same for every interaction. Each of us is receptive to a different mix of logos, ethos, and pathos, depending on our personal inclinations and the decision at hand.

Most enter the fundraising arena committed to using logic to win the day. After all, logic has the illusion of being "rational," "objective," and "unarguable." This idea didn't come out of nowhere; in fact, it's been a foundational assumption about our entire economic system. No less a thinker than Adam Smith formulated his thesis of capitalism on the assumption that people are rational and make rational decisions.[17]

Novice fundraisers, therefore, dutifully present all the logical reasons for investing in their project and completely ignore the other elements in play. However, most people, including investors, do not make investment decisions entirely based on logic. Logic needs to be present, but it has to fit the operating system of the person in front of you.

The truth is that investors, like the rest of us, often make decisions primarily based on ethos or pathos. Logos simply justifies the decision they want to make. Consider the pitch of the World Wildlife Fund for donations. At their fundraisers, they have pictures of cute seals and majestic tigers everywhere. They tell uplifting stories of the beautiful animals they've saved and tragic stories of the ones who are still suffering. The appeal isn't logical. There's no logical benefit for the individual investor in saving these animals. They write checks based on their values and their emotional reaction to pictures of those animals. Even though the loss of all Siberian tigers in the world wouldn't affect these donors at all, they feel that saving those animals is the "right thing to do." There's a persuasive logic underlying how the fund will use those donations to help the animals, but it's just a means of smoothing the path to a yes once the ethical and emotional arguments have done their work.

There are plenty of other examples of this throughout our lives, but for me, the ultimate proof that we aren't primarily rational, logical creatures is the topic of weight loss. Millions upon millions of people struggle with their weight. A gigantic industry has been created to address this issue. Of course, if humans were truly rational and behaved rationally, that industry would not exist. Obesity would occur only in those who are genetically predisposed to it and those whose socioeconomic conditions make it impossible to ingest healthier calories.

Everyone else is, in some sense, overweight by "choice." By that, I mean they've all had a conversation with themselves in which they acknowledge that they want to be thinner and healthier. They all know the value of losing their extra weight. There's value in the fact that it would improve their health. They'd feel better. They'd likely live longer. There are no more powerful values than those. And those aren't the only values at play. There are also societal values, which regularly promote health, muscles, and thinness as our standards of beauty. Those standards, as an aside, are entirely socially constructed. They are not universal. So the fact that our society constantly reminds us that we are beautiful only if we are thin and in good shape has a very potent egoic pull.

Further, we know logically how to achieve this goal. We all know the path to losing weight: move more, eat less. No one debates that. There's some nuance in this point—discussions about the best workout practices, the types of carbohydrates we should eat, and our schedule for eating—but the basic facts are well-established and well-known. Everyone who is overweight knows that if they walked more and ate better, they'd lose weight, and their logical and ethical arguments all lead to this being the right choice.

And yet most people don't do it. Why? Because of the power of the emotional argument within them. By *emotional argument*, I don't only mean things like happiness and sadness but also the feelings that arise within us through how our bodies *feel*. Those are very powerful forces. Our bodies want to relax. So, after a tough day, we often have an emotional desire to sit back and enjoy simple carbohydrates, such as ice cream. This is hardwired into our biology. Our ancestors lacked such easy access to those calories. After the stress of being chased by a rampaging wooly rhino, if such calories were available to replenish them, their bodies knew to feast. That preference remains so overwhelmingly powerful that it can easily overshadow all our logic and values. Again, there are no more compelling value systems than those that allow us to live better and live longer, but our population is nonetheless increasingly overweight.

This dynamic increases as we become more prosperous. In other words, the easier it is to attain those calories, the more we give in to them.

These same qualities can be found in investments in businesses. Investors might put their money in local restaurants to build up their community or agree to build affordable housing, even though it reduces their profits in return for ethical or emotional reward. I have often convinced investors to put money into projects that may never pay out because it could lead to cures for diseases or a far better world. Investors, like all people, want to be a part of a better future. That isn't a logical desire; it's an emotional and ethical one.

For all that, though, you can't trust that pathos and ethos will see you through without logos. Ignoring logos is dangerous for several reasons: Most significantly, logos is often the preferred method of explaining to others *why* you made the choice you did. As we saw in the last chapter, a logical statement is the easiest to repeat to others. Additionally, people can train themselves to counteract the persuasive power of those ethical and emotional elements, and many institutional investors do just that. It is possible to discipline yourself and create significant detachment from your emotional triggers. Those triggers still exist within these individuals, but they're buried deep within. This is what we mean when we say someone "has their guard up." Successful investors are often the ones who have the most formidable defenses to our ethical and emotional arguments.

Finally, even if emotion or values wins the day at first, a lack of logic can cause a project to unravel quickly once people have a chance to reset and reexamine your arguments. This is what happened to the Defund the Police movement: It over-indexed on pathos and ethos at the expense of logos. In the wake of the murder of George Floyd in 2020, there was genuine and justifiable outrage and an ethical need for some kind of change. Defund the Police captured this need and, for a short while, seemed to carry the argument. Eventually, though, it ran into the hard logic of why the police exist in the first place. Simply put, a democratic society needs to be able to enforce the laws of the people. For this *reason* (logos), public support slowly moved away from Defund the Police as emotion drained from the situation. The movement came to represent a lost opportunity. Regardless of one's stance on the subject, Defund the Police would have benefited enormously from following Aristotle's theory of rhetoric by emphasizing a sound alternative to public security.

Answer Their *Why*

Desire often manifests for the investor in a single word: *why*. When you get into the room, *why* is the biggest question on the investor's mind. Why you? Why now? Why this project? In short, why should they put their money where you want them to? Why not put it elsewhere?

As with everything else, you have to answer that *why* with logic, values, and emotion.

This is how I win over investors all the time. These days, I'm working on raising capital for research and development in AI. While there's a very strong logical argument that AI has a lot of potential for financial gain, I don't end my argument there. I also include ethical and emotional reasons that stoke the investor's desires.

I might hit an investor with an argument that centers on the ethics of their profession. I'll say something like,

"The internet. Wireless connections. Smartphones. Social media. Cloud computing. These were the big investment engines of the past thirty years. It would be *irresponsible* to miss out on this next major technological breakthrough."

Or I might turn that appeal to the values they want to see in society: "AI could end cancer, save the environment, and end hunger. Or AI could go wrong and really screw things up for America and the rest of the world. You have a duty to invest in a company (like mine) that is committed to developing this technology *responsibly and for the good of society.*"

At the same time, I might stoke their emotional excitement for this opportunity. "Think of the potential discoveries! Think of being an early investor in a once-in-a-lifetime innovation! This is the future, and you can be part of changing it for the better!"

Each element here drives deeper into *why* they need to invest with me *right now*. And as I see them focus more toward one element or the other, that clues me in to which argument most appeals to them in that moment. With that knowledge, I can turn the dial up on my pitch and max out their desire for this product.

Then, the only thing left to account for is the fear holding them back.

Chapter 7

Relieving Fear

N*o.*

It's the most common word you hear in fundraising. Even when you have the best product on the market, you will hear the word "no" with astonishing frequency.

Why do people say it? Assuming they want what you have on offer, why do they reject it? If you ask, often they'll give you a reason:

"I'm not sure this will make money."

"I don't want to waste my time when there could be better opportunities out there."

"There's just too much risk here."

We might label the emotional impulse behind these statements as insecurity, uncertainty, or doubt, but they all really come down to *fear. Fear is the source of no.* And if you want to get to yes, you have to address that root emotion as much as you address desire.

The Flipside of Desire

Desire and fear are the yin and yang of decision-making. They make up two parts of a whole. We see this not just in fundraising but in religious and moral codes throughout history that seek to regulate our behavior. There's the desire to get to heaven and the fear of going to hell. There's the desire for nirvana and the fear of the eternal cycles of rebirth of Samsara. There's the desire for a bountiful harvest blessed by the gods and the fear of a famine or flood when angering them.

In each system, fear and desire are always equal and opposite forces compelling us toward a certain action. Our internal decision-making processes always put these two emotions at odds. We desire life, so we fear death. We desire status, so we fear embarrassment. We desire comfort, so we fear poverty. We desire wealth, so we fear being cheated.

In persuasion, you have to speak to both of these forces. Too often, though, fundraisers ignore fear entirely. They focus on why an investor *should* do something and fail to address the counterargument—*why they're afraid to do it.*

If anything, fundraisers should concentrate *more* on this latter point. Fear is our master emotion, and we should respect it. It has primacy over our behavior because it's what keeps us safe and out of trouble. At the least sign of danger, it sets off our fight-or-flight instinct.

We may not *enjoy* the shock of a fear response, but it is absolutely vital in our survival. In a certain sense, the primary reason we are here is that our ancestors developed a keen awareness of threats and the means to respond to them.

Originally, this impulse was focused on physical danger, but as we've evolved, our egos have expanded the remit of the amygdala, the part of the brain that enables us to experience emotions. In the modern world, fear is no longer *just* triggered by what could physically kill or injure us. The same impulses fire over things that might harm our identity. We feel fear (as well as its partners: worry, concern, anxiety, and so on) when our reputation is at risk. We fret over how our actions are perceived by others or if we've made the right decision when committing to a new job. This fear is centered on our sense of self and how others regard us. We also fear great losses to our finances or comfort. These losses don't usually result in death, but they are costly in a modern society.

Thus, we need to have a healthy amount of such fear to protect our identity as we interact with our community. And due to the high-risk nature of investment, an investor needs more fear than most people. They may be investing large resources, but those resources are finite. They're under immense pressure to invest well and to spur significant growth. They live under constant fear of fraud, fear of underperforming, fear of overexposure, fear of failure, and fear of missing out on a major opportunity.

You have to help them overcome these fears to gain access to the investment you're seeking. The investor's fears are a series of locked doors behind which they hide their desire for investment. Those doors will remain locked unless you are able to relieve those fears. Fear is the great barrier: It doesn't matter how great your product is or how much people want it if they are too scared to act.

Once you activate someone's sympathetic nervous system, which is responsible for our fight-or-flight response, you undermine your ability to persuade. When an investor reaches that state, you are no longer dealing with a fully functioning human. The frontal lobe and the ego recede, and the animalistic hindbrain takes over. This is why, when people get cornered in an argument, many double down even when it's unreasonable. They're fighting back without much control from their more logical frontal lobe.

The only way out of this is to activate the parasympathetic nervous system to calm them down. This is the "rest and digest" process, a time-out that allows people to catch their breath and return to normal. In fundraising, we have to focus on reducing the stress that activates the amygdala and sympathetic nervous system, creating a calming environment that keeps the parasympathetic nervous system in the driver's seat.

With this in mind, look again at the Persuasion Equation from the previous chapter:

Persuasion = Desire − Fear

Persuasion only happens after you subtract fear from desire. If you have a negative balance, then the person's fear will remain greater than their desire. At that point, it doesn't matter how good the offer is. The answer will always remain no.

The Cialdini Method

Trust is your best tool in the effort to relieve fear. It is a natural balm to fear, offering the brain a reason to engage the parasympathetic nervous system and de-escalate. This has roots in our evolution. In a prehistoric world, we would have feared nearly everything—with good reason. The only reason to reduce fear would be to trust in certain people, locations, and objects. If an authority in your tribe said a path would be safe, you would likely trust the path. If everyone in the tribe agreed that a berry was nontoxic, you'd probably eat it. And so on.

This same relationship between trust and fear is in place today. Chris Fussell, a former Navy SEAL and current lecturer at Yale University, once shared a story with me about General Stanley McChrystal during his time as commander of US forces in Afghanistan. A meeting was scheduled with various tribal leaders in the country. The standard practice for the US military was for our leaders to be as protected as possible. We couldn't afford to lose them in an unexpected attack. But McChrystal took a different path. He was the first general to go to a meeting like that without any body armor. He came in as unprotected as those tribal leaders. In other words, he demonstrated that he trusted them, and he received trust in return.[18]

If you can inspire trust in an investor, you can reduce their fear—and thus allow desire to sway their decision. The question at this point, then, is obvious: How do you create that trust?

There's something to be said for leading with trust, as McChrystal did. For the most part, though, the answer is the Cialdini Method.[19]

Named after psychologist and professor Robert Cialdini, the Cialdini Method is, in many ways, a descendant of logos, ethos, and pathos. You might consider it one strand of innovation that can be traced back to those initial insights from Aristotle. In the same way calculus gave us physics, which gave us an understanding of the nature of movement, which in turn unlocked our understand of how a bird flies, how light works, and the nature of atomic reactions—so too has logos, ethos, and pathos led to numerous philosophical, psychological, and technological innovations in the understanding of the mind. It's led to many offshoots of research and insight, and Robert Cialdini is at the end of one line of inquiry into influence and persuasion.

While a professor in the Department of Psychology at Arizona State University, Cialdini wrote the groundbreaking book *Influence: The Psychology of Persuasion*. In this eye-opening book, Cialdini documents how and why the human condition responds to various interactions. As he describes it, the human brain is inundated with information all the time. To sort through this information and act appropriately, the mind uses default frameworks that allow it to make decisions.[20] For our purposes, I've condensed and reorganized his concepts slightly into six categories:

- Authority
- Consensus
- Reciprocity

- Consistency
- Liking
- Scarcity

These default systems exist across human society, although some societies emphasize one framework or another over the others.

In *Influence*, Cialdini initially attempted to simply explain the nature of these frameworks. As he did so, however, he realized that marketing professionals had been using these same frameworks as trapdoors into persuading their customers. A set of defaults originally evolved to ensure our survival now allowed masters of marketing to persuade us to buy their products. And understanding those same frameworks can allow you to reduce the investor's instinctive fear and preference for no.

Let's delve more deeply into each one.

Authority

Authority is perhaps the most obvious element of persuasion that Cialdini developed. We see its power everywhere. We look up to authorities because our survival hinges on their success. Again, this is why our ancestors trusted and felt less fearful when the chief of their tribe told them that a path was safe. They were the authority. Authorities are the people we have empowered to keep us safe, and so we tend to comply with their recommendations.

Authority is not only given to those in positions of leadership; it also extends to experts. Crucially, this is the more persuasive form of Authority in fundraising. While you can leverage Authority through power, you do not have that power in your relationship with the investor. You aren't a colonel commanding a lieutenant to march into battle or a four-star general in charge of the most powerful military in the world meeting with tribal elders. If anything, the investor has more of that sort of Authority than you do. The only Authority you have access to as a fundraiser is your expertise in the investment you want them to make with you. Luckily, this can still be an effective use of the Rule of Authority.

When we believe someone knows more than we do about a particular subject, we naturally seek their wisdom and guidance. In our primitive state, we would have sought them out to teach us to hunt, grow food, raise children, or fight. Today, we go to them for medical and legal advice. We take their word on what medications we should use and whether we have a personal injury case. We have an innate sense that we should listen to and trust these people.

This is why you hear that "four out of five dentists approve" of Trident gum in advertising, why we submit references when applying for a position, and why businesses put out original research and white papers. It's about building Authority in a certain area. It's establishing experience and a track record. It all goes to creating a sense of authoritative expertise.

It's also why my biography is included in this book. It shows you that I'm an authority on fundraising whom you naturally want to trust. This Authority helps me persuade you to put aside your skepticism and trust my ideas.

If you can establish yourself as an expert authority in your investment space, then you will increase your ability to diminish the investor's fears. They will therefore have less uncertainty when considering an investment.

If you are among the top experts in your space—say, the CEO of a prominent company with a proven track record or a tech wizard at the forefront of a new industry—this is perhaps the most powerful tool in your bag for relieving investor fear. Sam Altman has done this very successfully, leveraging OpenAI's early breakthroughs in artificial intelligence. Before him, Elon Musk was able to use his authority as a tech visionary from PayPal, and then Tesla, and then SpaceX to raise billions.

For those who lack the Authority of expertise you can often borrow some. If you are connected to the subject matter expert in your area, their endorsement gives you Authority. Because the expert trusts you, some of their Authority rubs off.

Be aware, though, that the greater the distance from the expert, the less Authority available. In other words, the weaker your relationship with the authority, the less Authority you get to borrow. Equally, the less expertise or renown the expert possesses, the less Authority you can receive from them, no matter how close you are.

Borrowed Authority is like the gravitational pull of planets in orbit. The closer the planet is to you, the more powerful the pull. Likewise, the larger the planet, the more powerful the pull.

Imagine you have some connection to a Jupiter-like Authority: a very successful investor who is *the* authority in a particular space. He could have any number of relationships with you and your fund. He might be a former colleague or a onetime mentor for a brief period. He might endorse your product, put some money into the fund himself, consult with your company, be part of the team, or run the whole enterprise. The closer you are to that authority, the stronger their gravitational pull.

Let's make this more concrete. This time, imagine you run a skateboarding company looking for investment, and you have two potential sources of Authority: well-known skateboarding legend Tony Hawk and Yuto Horigome, the current number one skateboarder in the world (who you have probably never heard of). These are the Jupiter and Saturn of the skateboarding world. Given the choice, you'd probably prefer to mention Hawk if he has a particularly close relationship with your business. Everyone knows who he is, even if they know nothing about skateboarding. He has a successful series of video games with his name on them, after all. But what creates more Authority for you in the room: saying Tony Hawk likes your board after giving one a spin or saying Horigome himself designed the board?

There's no easy answer to that choice. The answer depends on the project, the name, and the investor.

Consensus

Of course, in reality, you'd mention both Tony Hawk and Yuto Horigome in your pitch—because this would not only build Authority but also create the perception of Consensus, another element of Cialdini's framework.

Like Authority, the Rule of Consensus (which Cialdini refers to as "social proof") speaks to the primary frameworks we use for survival. If you were in the woods and saw everyone else running the other direction, what would you do? You'd turn and run in the same direction as the others. It's your natural instinct, for good reason. Our ancestors who didn't turn to run with the pack—those who kept walking the other direction—found out there was a bear in the woods. Their genes didn't survive the mistake.

This is why we trust the wisdom of the masses. Perhaps your mother once asked, "If all your friends jumped off a bridge, would you do it too?" Not only would most of us do it, but our natural instinct would tell us we *should* do it. If everyone is jumping off a bridge, it suggests that's the safer option. In this scenario, there may be a Consensus that staying on the bridge is actually more dangerous.

For all that, I think people perceive the Rule of Consensus as a less impressive tool than it really is. When used to full effect, it is one of the most powerful forms of persuasion possible. Consensus is the essential aim of propaganda. And like propaganda, it has the potential to do what few other tools can: get you to stop thinking.

Consensus thinking even leads to people rejecting cold, hard scientific data. One such example is the initial resistance to the aforementioned theory of heliocentrism, which states the Sun is the center of our solar system. When Copernicus proposed this theory in the sixteenth century, the prevailing belief was that Earth was the center of the universe (geocentrism). Despite observational data supporting heliocentrism, such as the phases of Venus and the retrograde motion of planets, many in the scientific and religious communities rejected these findings due to deeply ingrained philosophical and theological views.

Consensus is so powerful because we need it not just for our protection but to build community. In general, we follow the mores and preferences of our community because it creates cohesion across our tribe and provides us with an individual sense of belonging. When society lacks the cohesion of Consensus, stress and tension increase as neighbors stop trusting one another—a situation we've all witnessed over the past decade.

Everywhere you look, Consensus glues society together. Indeed, without it, we tend to come unglued. Our entire global financial system is predicated on a Consensus that the US dollar has unique, hegemonic power to hold the entire world economy together. That faith is based on some truth but is largely sustained by Consensus. And that Consensus is so strong that even some of the other largest, strongest countries in the world—China, Russia, and Saudi Arabia, to name a few—have been unable to dislodge it.

This is why communities tend to share the same politics and behaviors. Consensus is central to our sense of morals and ethics. We believe things are right and wrong because everyone around us believes that. Most of the time, we simply follow along.

Next time you're in a debate about something—anything, really—look out for the use of "everybody" entering the discussion. "Everybody agrees that we should lower interest rates." "Everyone knows that New York has the best pizza." "Everybody thinks your tardiness is a problem in this department."

This is such a common and tempting tactic because we all instinctively reach for Consensus to win an argument. If everyone truly does feel or think a certain way, we feel a deep need to agree—to stop thinking and stop fighting against the tide. We can't exist in a civilization unless we care about other people's opinions. When others agree about something, we feel we ought to agree . . . or we are scared to disagree.

Consensus is not an all-powerful impulse, of course. We often laud the value of taking "the road less traveled by."[21] But we celebrate it because it is so difficult and rare. We might take that road at one time or another in our lives, but often only for a single conscientious decision—an individual moment when we choose to act against Consensus.

Investors, as a general rule, do not like the road less traveled. Quite the opposite: Consensus is particularly prized in investment. Consensus suggests that an investment is safe. And when the stakes are so high, safety is a priority.

Nowhere is such Consensus more valued than in the meritocratic world of institutional money, such as banks, pension funds, hedge funds, and insurance companies. Most institutional money is invested by committees. Committees offer the best governance because they consist of multiple people who can stress-test an idea before it enters the investment pool. It's rare to see a decision-making body support a contrarian idea. A Consensus process, by its very nature, is designed to find Consensus thinking. To convince such a committee to take a contrarian position, it must be extremely obvious. That's a tautology, though, because if your position is that obvious, almost by definition, you can no longer be the contrarian option. You've already become the Consensus!

The easiest way around this catch is to avoid it entirely. You can seek out investors who are unchallenged by a committee—whose hands are free to take on the contrarian position and who want to assume the risk of the path less traveled by. Money controlled in monarchic systems is often far easier to convince because the need for Consensus is lower. That's not to say all kingdoms would entertain riskier investments, but some may.

In tribal systems, though, be wary of creating polarization around your product. Consensus can win over some of the remaining holdouts, but if others *negatively polarize* against you, that may be the end of your chance to win over the room. Once polarization happens, people can become quite stubborn over what they believe to be "right," and all discussion ends.

If you do seek institutional investment, be prepared to use other tools of persuasion to overcome their reticence, and brace yourself for a lot of failure. I have successfully persuaded many committees of the value of a particular fund, only for them to vote no anyway because they felt it was outside their mandate. That still happens to me today.

To have any chance at all under those circumstances, you have to design your pitch to offer the kind of logos, ethos, and pathos persuasion that overwhelms the committee's fears of voting for the contrarian choice. This requires "if the glove does not fit, you must acquit" levels of persuasion. If you can give them a powerful line or story they can use to explain their decision that speaks to something they deeply desire (and also follows most of their most important rules), there's a small chance you can get a win.

This line might have to do with building up their community, lifting up a minority owner, or creating a unique upside for their marketing. If you're seeking investment for a restaurant, for instance, you might emphasize the lack of Black ownership in the community, for instance, or the unique potential for the restaurant to spin off into a chain.

That could be enough to overcome their fearful reticence to invest. But the bigger the investment, the more powerful this persuasion has to be. And the odds are always going to be against you.

Reciprocity

According to Cialdini, Reciprocity underpins all our ethics. To see this, look no further than the Golden Rule: "Do unto others as you would have them do unto you." That rule is *golden* because it's foundational. It exists in every religious moral code. It's there in Buddhism, Hinduism, Judaism, Christianity, and Islam. It's also inherent in our sense of justice and fairness, which informs our legal system.

You even find it in the Beatles: "The love you take is equal to the love you make."[22]

This is a core assumption of civilization. What you put in, you get out. When humans come together, we reciprocate, seeking to offer and take in equal measure. Anyone who takes without reciprocating either ends up on the edges of society or, ironically, at the head of it. Regardless, it's considered nonstandard behavior.

Reciprocity is our standard because it grounds our expectations in every type of relationship, whether in tribes, teams, organizations, or families. All business transactions require this same sense of Reciprocity. I give something (often money), and you give me something in return (a service or a product).

This is biologically built into the human character. And not just humans. In one study, two monkeys were placed in a cage where they could see food in a container. Neither monkey, however, could open it without the help of the other. What happened? They worked together to get the jar and open it. And once it was open, they split the treat evenly.[23]

If produced from a place of genuine generosity and communal interest, Reciprocity is one of the most authentic and persuasive tools available. This technique is so powerful that we actually place legal barriers around it. Take Reciprocity too far—or use it for the wrong ends—and it becomes a bribe.

The reason for the legal limits is that Reciprocity can remove fear from the equation. It turns fear into acceptance by creating a sense of obligation. We have laws against bribing judges because we need judges to fear losing their jobs and going to jail for indulging in Reciprocity with those on trial. Otherwise, bribing judges would be more common, and that would lead to every criminal with deep pockets being pretty sure of an acquittal. In fact, it's not hard to find justice systems around the world with weak enforcement mechanisms where this exact thing takes place.

We have a natural desire to return a gift or favor, and that desire often overcomes our fear. Remember, we're hardwired to reciprocate. And normative behavior demands that the greater our sense of debt, the more we will give. People will give away billions out of a sense of obligation and Reciprocity to a particular community. They'll give their very lives in the name of Reciprocity to their country.

To create this sense of Reciprocity, you must seek out opportunities to give a little more to those you are doing business with. Can you provide a service, a favor, or a kindness to the person in the room? What do they need that you can offer them? Is there information they need? A compromise they are struggling to reach? Perhaps there's some perk you could provide that would make their day a little more enjoyable.

If you're raising money for that hypothetical restaurant mentioned above, you can offer to leave a table free for them whenever they come in. Maybe you could give them free drinks on every visit. What we often call the "VIP treatment" is really a form of Reciprocity—giving them something for their money.

But you have to be careful to get the balance right here. Go too far, and Reciprocity becomes a bribe. Fail to go far enough, and you can create resentment. It's very possible to assume you have done a favor when the other person in the room doesn't see it that way. For example, when I stay at a nice hotel, I often receive a request to fill out a survey afterward. I find this deeply annoying. I have already given them money in exchange for their comfortable room. They have not done anything for me that puts me under further obligation. If they want more from me, they have to *offer* me more first. Otherwise, they are breaking the Rules of Reciprocation, and I'm less likely to stay there next time.

The same can be true in fundraising. Taking an investor to the Super Bowl is more than just building a relationship. It is a nice way of creating Reciprocity. However, some people are turned off by an invitation of that magnitude, as they may not want to feel more obliged to do something for you, such as take a meeting, listen to a pitch, or even give you money. Likewise, be careful placing yourself under obligation. Some people use this rule to exert control. "I did this for you," they may say, "so now you owe me." That obligation can then become a permanent debt to be cashed in whenever and however they choose.

This is what happens at the beginning of *The Godfather*, as a man begs Don Corleone for revenge. Two men have beaten the man's daughter, and the furious father wants the Godfather to mete out reciprocal justice. He initially attempts direct Reciprocity for this act, saying he will give Don Corleone anything, trying to pay for this service, but this offends the Godfather.

Instead, Don Corleone wants something more ambiguous, and in many ways, more unsettling. "Someday," he says, "and that day may never come, I may call upon you to do a service for me."

That demand is far greater than any fee the Godfather could have requested. The cost is a lifetime of debt. To get his justice, the father will be obligated for life.[24]

Consistency

Next up in our tour of Cialdini's framework is Consistency, which is all about saying what you mean, meaning what you say, and doing what you mean. In *Influence*, Cialdini focuses this principle on how each of us feels a need to be consistent in our own behavior. Here, we will focus on a different aspect of the principle: how our consistent behavior influences investors.

If Reciprocity is the foundation of human cooperation, then Consistency is the glue. As prehistoric man gathered into tribes, consistent behavior was an output of cultural norms, because it created the important predictability that humans need to work in teams and align their goals and objectives. Moreover, Consistency simplified human interaction, which allowed people to make quicker judgments—a useful trait in chaotic and threatening situations.

Consistency also increases the sense that we can trust someone. Whether in tribal, ancient, or modern society, erratic behavior in a leader or someone in a position of responsibility creates the potential for negative outcomes we can't prepare for. To put it another way, we are able to trust someone because we know the history of their behavior. If their behavior shows a consistent pattern and we approve of that pattern, we trust them to make similar decisions in the future. Consistency allows us to predict outcomes.

In fundraising, this is often distilled down to your track record. If you have a history of providing value to investors and living up to your word, you will have the next investor's trust. And that trust, once again, reduces their fear.

Consider Warren Buffett. When he backs a product, everyone listens because he's consistently backed winners. Investors don't walk into a meeting with Buffett fearful that they'll lose their money or that Buffett will lie or exaggerate to convince them to invest. They know they can trust him.

Consistency can take a lifetime to build but just a moment to destroy. One overstatement of a product's potential, one failed promise, and it can disappear. You can also lose it over a single sales cycle. While in the act of persuasion, everything you say has to be consistent. You can't keep making up new stories or complicating things. Every time you do, you lose trust.

This is why politicians dread being accused of *flip-flopping*, or inexplicably reversing a previously stated position. At best, it suggests inconsistency, which erodes trust. At worst, it suggests hypocrisy, which erodes likability—a topic I will discuss below.

The consequences of this accusation can be devastating to a political career. During the 2004 presidential election, Senator John Kerry was accused of flip-flopping on several key issues, most notably his stance on the Iraq War. This perceived inconsistency was leveraged by opponents to portray him as unreliable and indecisive.[25] Additionally, Kerry faced scrutiny on issues such as health care and taxes, where his positions appeared to shift over time, contributing to the narrative of flip-flopping that became a central theme in his opponent's campaign.[26] The result was that an otherwise capable politician never got to sit in the Oval Office.

If you lack a track record, you can build Consistency slowly by making small promises and following through. These can relate to your product, but they don't have to. Earlier in my career, I used to send books to clients. If a book came up naturally in conversation, I would promise to send it to them. Afterward, I would make a point of sending it the same day with a little note mentioning our encounter. They probably never read beyond the note, but it showed I was paying attention and that I did what I said—and did it quickly.

Likewise, if someone emails and you consistently get back to them quickly, it shows them that they are important to you and that you are reliable and trustworthy. However, if you regularly take days to respond, it communicates the exact opposite.

Whether across a whole career or a short exchange of emails, never underestimate how much Consistency alleviates fear in investors. When people believe you'll do what you say, they're far more likely to believe your investment opportunity is as impressive as you claim.

Liking

You probably don't need Cialdini to tell you that persuasion is easier when the other person in the room likes you. However, the topic is a bit more complex than that obvious point suggests.

As we've already covered in chapter 4, you want people to like you because if they like you, they'll pay attention to you. They'll also tend to trust you. This is likely hardwired into our DNA as the "I like you/I am like you" dynamic that feeds into the effectiveness of cooperation and community among humans.

Take the first element of that equation—"I like you." It is plainly obvious that charismatic individuals have a certain advantage over others when commanding attention and interest. That's not to say charm is a perfect hack to persuasion. I'm sure we can all think of people we *like* but don't *trust*. Charisma can take you a long way precisely because people will be predisposed to set aside fear and listen to you, but it doesn't guarantee trust. The real power lies in maintaining attention and what you do with it. If someone likes you, they're more likely to return your email, answer the phone, and invite you into the room. They'll spend that little bit of extra time listening to you—and that can give you the access you need to reduce fear, raise desire, and persuade them.

One way to do this is by doubling down on the other side of the equation—"I am like you"—through *mirroring*. Mirroring is a powerful communication technique in which one person subtly imitates the gestures, speech patterns, or emotional expressions of another. This technique fosters trust by creating a sense of rapport and connection. When individuals observe similar body language or vocal tones, they often feel more comfortable and understood. By reflecting the feelings and behaviors of others, mirroring demonstrates empathy and attentiveness, which can lead to deeper emotional bonds. This alignment in nonverbal communication signals agreement and validation, making others feel valued and recognized. As a result, mirroring not only enhances likability but also encourages openness, which is essential when convincing someone to consider your idea or change their mind.

This sense of similarity creates a feeling that we are in the same community, that we belong to the same tribe, and that we want to support others in our community. Communities are often founded on shared values and, at least in the past, shared ethnic histories. Everyone was, in a very literal sense, like everyone else. Tapping into such old instincts for building community can be a powerful force.

Again, this is not foolproof. I know many people I am like whom I do not trust (and who perhaps don't trust me). But it does increase the space for trust and decrease the room for fear to expand. That can open the door for desire to take the lead.

Scarcity

There's one final framework in the Cialdini Method I want to cover here, but it's somewhat distinct from the others. This is the only framework that involves *using* fear to *reduce* fear. And it's particularly potent—in positive and negative ways—for the investor. I'm talking about Scarcity.

Scarcity is a permanent mindset, one we are all living in—at least in some respect. What we fear being or becoming scarce varies depending on the person. The most prominent example is money. Have you ever noticed that even when you get a raise, you still feel you don't have enough? That's because in this mindset, there's never enough.

Others feel a Scarcity of affection. To see this, just look at how your dog behaves. They can never get enough of your attention. That's how many people feel—there's never enough love for them to feel they have enough.

Many people in the fundraising and finance worlds feel a Scarcity of recognition or status. They want respect. They want to be known for their brilliance. Even once they are lauded for their success, as soon as the limelight turns elsewhere, they fear it'll never come back.

My Scarcity mindset revolves around time. I'll move items in my drawers just so I can reach things without wasting a couple of seconds the next time I walk across a room. I'll actually part with money in order to ensure my time isn't wasted. I even eat dehydrated foods for lunch. I heat one up for two minutes, and it gives me all the nutrients I need. And it tastes . . . pretty poor, actually. The irony is that I can afford to eat anything, and I live in Brooklyn, which is one of the best places in the world to find great food on every street. But it would take an extra half hour to do that, and I fear losing that time.

This feeling of Scarcity lurks within each of us because we're programmed with it. Scarcity in nature connects to death. For prehistoric humans, the possibility that there wasn't enough food or clean water instilled fear, which was crucial for survival.

As fundraisers, we can utilize Scarcity in persuasion in two ways: either to alleviate the other person's fear or to stoke it to our advantage. The most common way to stoke fear is through what's been popularized in recent years as the fear of missing out, or FOMO.

FOMO is a very effective and easy lever to pull when trying to persuade someone. We see it all the time in advertising:

- "Call now while supplies last!"
- "Don't miss out on this incredible deal!"
- "Sale ends Friday, so hurry in before it's too late!"

These pitches all play up the fear of missing some deal or experience. They literally *advertise* Scarcity.

FOMO is a particularly potent fear in the funding arena. No investor wants to miss out on the next big thing—or even the next *moderately successful* thing. One reason why FOMO is such a strong motivator is that the fear of missing out isn't *just* one fear. In fact, many fears are wrapped up in someone's FOMO—a fear of losing wealth, a fear of losing face, a fear of being laughed at, a fear of failure, a fear of missing a "once-in-a-lifetime" opportunity, a fear of being in the wrong place at the wrong time, and so on. You can imagine how easy it is to trigger this fear in the other person in the room. Once triggered, the investor will often set aside other considerations to focus on reducing their fear of missing out.

But be forewarned, there's a dark side to this technique. This is the same motivation that creates bubbles in the market. It's what fuels the sudden surge in Bitcoin's value or real estate prices before a crash. FOMO creates a pile-on effect as everyone tries to get in on something before it's too late—but pumping up any product like that is unsustainable.

Additionally, FOMO has a "half-life," where the effect eventually wears off. The only way to avoid this is to keep feeding the fear. If I don't want to invest and you scare me into doing it, I may come to regret the decision as soon as the fear dissipates. The only way to push off the risk of regret is to build fear indefinitely. This is a nearly impossible task and, in my experience, is where honest people can be tempted to defraud others in order to buy enough time to finally find success.

This is how Ponzi schemes get started. In this scenario, an original group of investors puts money in, but success doesn't come as promised. So, a shady fundraiser or entrepreneur promises a new group of investors an even greater return. Those new investors put in a pile of money, and the fundraiser uses those proceeds to provide a (fake) return to the original investors. This creates the illusion of a good investment, because the early investors *seem* to have made their promised return.

Other people see the original investors making money as promised, and suddenly they're clamoring to invest in the fund "before it's too late." The fundraiser uses *their* funds to pay (fake) returns to the previous group of investors, and the cycle keeps repeating. This spiral of FOMO investment continues until either someone discovers the scheme or the fundraiser burns through the pool of potential investors. Once new money stops entering the system, the whole sham falls apart . . . fast.

You can also employ Scarcity in a different way: by making *yourself* scarce. This can have the effect of suggesting you're busy, important, and therefore have more Authority. But this, too, can backfire. In the first place, people may begin to escalate their problems in order to secure your attention. That can create a climate of drama, with every problem categorized as a catastrophe to get your attention. And this, in turn, can create a climate of fear across the organization. Mishandled, such climates can put companies in great distress.

A legendary example of this phenomenon is the tale of former Yahoo CEO Marissa Mayer. She was recruited in 2012 from Google, where she had a reputation for being a strong and innovative leader. However, once she arrived at Yahoo, people began to notice that she maintained her distance and did not communicate broadly the rationale for many of the acquisitions Yahoo made under her leadership. She made herself scarce.

In the following years, workers reported that they felt disconnected from the company's leadership and direction. They felt sidelined, leading to a culture of confusion and resentment. Ultimately, Mayer's inaccessibility and the resulting internal drama contributed to a decline in morale at Yahoo, which struggled to retain talent and innovate during her tenure. That contributed significantly to their fall from internet dominance.[27]

Personal scarcity also invites those with dominant personalities to go after you. For those who need to feel in control, your scarcity is a threat. They will see how you control your time, and they will pressure you to give up that control. They might schedule important meetings and force you to break other commitments, or they may create a Scarcity standoff in which they try to make *you* chase after *them*.

Ultimately, FOMO in fundraising is something like the One Ring in *The Lord of the Rings*. It can be powerful and, in theory, lead to positive outcomes, but it also has the outsized potential to turn otherwise positive outcomes negative. It's hard to master and use it authentically without surrendering to the darker side of manipulation.

It's far better, then, to recognize Scarcity and help the other person in the room reduce it. I often play down Scarcity in my work—even exaggerating the *abundance* of opportunity for the funds I represent. (Abundance is Scarcity's polar opposite.)

When I do employ Scarcity, it's as a means of introducing what some people call *co-creation*. We'll further develop this idea later in the book. For now, you can understand co-creation as the act of working toward a shared aim with shared benefit. In co-creation, you work with the other person in the room to develop a solution that empowers you both. In this instance, you work together to find a solution that relieves the fear of Scarcity.

Respect and trust are often built from solving for fear, and, in my experience, this approach invites higher-quality, longer-term investors to the table. For instance, there's a common experience in fundraising that occurs after you've won over the investor and they're on board. It's called *buyer's remorse*. They suddenly realize something is still wrong. This usually happens when someone feels uncertain about the logos, ethos, or pathos of their investment.

Making a decision based on the emotional fear of missing out is not the problem. The problem arises when the Scarcity inherent in the process short-circuits the investor's logos and ethos. In other words, buyer's remorse is almost always an internal signal that something logically or ethically doesn't feel right about the decision. This is one of the important reasons why Scarcity tends not to be a long-term, sustainable approach to selling.

Some fundraisers might ignore this discomfort—after all, they've secured the investment. That was their job. I take a different approach. I work with those investors to co-create a solution *around* their buyer's remorse. Perhaps we need to decrease their investment in this project. Perhaps we need to find some further assurances. Whatever is necessary, we find a solution together. That can turn a one-time investor into a lifelong investment partner.

Reducing Your Own Fear

The Cialdini Method is a framework, not a guarantee. It is one of many tools you can use to speak to the deeper motivations within an investor in order to calm their fears. But as with much of the Tao, the value is in having a system to rely on. To function in this world, we need things we believe in. We need to believe the world works in a certain way and that we can operate a certain way within it. Otherwise, we lose confidence and trust in ourselves and our ability to act in various situations.

When you're in the room, you need a system that responds to investor fears not just for the straightforward reason that you must respond to them but because in having a system, you reduce your own fear. You speak from a place of certainty and confidence, which creates a fear-free climate.

This is a powerful tool to master not just in business but in life. For example, a true martial arts master is less likely to get into a fight not only because they have techniques to reduce risk but because they are confident enough in their abilities to keep a clear head when the risk of a fight occurs. They project that confidence, which reduces risk. They are able to be assertive without being aggressive, and most of the time, no one ever throws a punch.

That same confidence in your abilities to answer the investor's needs in the room makes you far more convincing and far less in need of techniques to reduce fear in the first place. No one trusts a nervous salesperson. Presenting with confidence goes a long way toward building trust, which is at the center of reversing investor fear.

Chapter 8

The Drama Triangle

In 1968, Stephen B. Karpman made one of those profound discoveries—one that changed how we look at human nature. His "Drama Triangle" suggested that, in conflict, we place every party into one of three roles: hero (rescuer), villain (persecutor), or victim (sufferer).[28] Once you absorb this idea, you see it everywhere: in family drama, TV drama, work drama, and, frankly, throughout all of human history.

Drama is everywhere in life because it is our natural response to encountering pain or the risk of pain. What Karpman discovered was that we turn all this drama into a play of sorts in our heads. Just think about your reaction when you stub your toe. Immediately, you feel like the universe is against you and that "stupid table" jumped in your way with the intent of ruining your day. This is your brain in action, dramatizing a state of affairs to create a narrative and characters to explain your feelings—even when some of those characters are inanimate.

Essentially, when something goes wrong—or may go wrong—we feel like victims. As *victims*, we seek a *villain*, and we look for a *hero* to save us from the situation. We dramatize our powerlessness and cast our eyes around for a rescuer. We see this in politics all the time. If the price of gas goes up or the economy flags, we immediately look to the president to step in as our hero—even though the president likely has limited ability to influence these economic forces, particularly in the short term.

This default setting is the product of the hindbrain, frontal lobe, and ego working together to see a threat and create a story around that threat in order to lead us to a potential solution. The hindbrain experiences some sort of fear, the frontal lobe creates a story about that fear, and the ego casts the roles, usually placing us in the starring role as the victim in need of rescue.

Applied to fundraising, when the person in the room feels fear in relation to your pitch, they dramatize the situation, turning themselves into a victim and you into the villain who is forcing them into this position. To relieve themself of this feeling, they may either turn on you or demand that you transform into the hero and somehow remove this drama.

This dramatized response is powerful and should not be underestimated. In the world beyond the room, the Drama Triangle can lead to some extreme forms of behavior. Indeed, it has long been the mechanism perpetrators unknowingly use to justify antisocial behaviors such as bullying, manipulation, dependency, spying, nonconsensual control, and even martyrdom.

But if you understand the sources and power of drama, instead of destroying a deal, it could seal it.

Hero, Villain, Victim

Recently, I learned an investor wanted to get me on the phone so he could yell at me. You might assume this caused me real distress. After all, who likes getting yelled at? In reality, though, I received the news in a positive light. I saw this moment as an opportunity. His anger would give me insight into who he is, what he fears, and what he needs from me for our partnership to be successful.

I understood that he saw me as a villain in his Drama Triangle, which also told me that he saw himself as a victim. Thanks to this knowledge, I could turn the encounter to my advantage. Like a judo master, the harder someone comes at me, the more power and force there is for me to redirect. Though he intended to put me on my back, I knew how to flip the circumstances.

The key to flipping these dynamics to your advantage is to understand that *anyone* can assume *any role* in the Drama Triangle. A boss can be our hero for offering us the afternoon off when we have a headache or a villain for keeping us late on a Friday. Depending on our circumstances and inclinations, we can make a villain out of government overreach, systemic racism, or a thoughtless neighbor who plays music too loudly late at night. Our heroes might be a politician, a church, a movement, or an aunt who always cooks a wonderful meal when we come over every other Sunday.

In each of the examples above, we cast a second role at the same time we place someone else in the position to be a hero or villain. We consistently place ourselves in the role of victim, being either rescued or tormented by others.

Like the rest of us, investors innately enter this same triangle when drama arises in their lives. Such drama is inevitable in fundraising, as it always is when money is involved.

Without understanding the Karpman Drama Triangle, it would be easy to misplay these situations. Greater mastery of these dynamics, though, offers the potential for deeper understanding of the other person in the room. Once you learn to recognize the Drama Triangle as it arises, you can become an expert at dissecting the drama, gaining more knowledge of the investor than they mean to share.

The Power and Risk of Villains and Heroes

Knowing the power of the Karpman Drama Triangle, your instinct here may be to lean into becoming the hero. After all, there is nobility and control in being a hero, and there are so many ways to place yourself in that position when you know what you're doing.

If you unfortunately fall into the role of the villain, it's often not hard to find a better candidate to fill that nefarious role, allowing you to jump into action as the hero to help solve the problem for your investor. If the investor reveals a different villain other than yourself, you could double down on the empathy card and pile on in solidarity, potentially fueling a martyrdom scenario that works to your benefit. In all these circumstances, *hero framing* would open up the opportunity to resolve the issue and create a powerful sense of obligation on the part of the investor. Who doesn't want to pay back their heroes for all the good work they've done?

This is, undeniably, an option when dealing with the Drama Triangle, but it is one that I counsel against. The short-term potential here is immense, but, not unlike using FOMO to relieve fear, it can have some unsustainable and far-from-ideal consequences.

To be clear, this is a form of manipulation, one that is most easily used on the desperate. It works well when someone needs to *find* a hero or needs to *be* a hero to solve a problem. It's instinctively easy to see how selling false promises works well on people who are suffering and have lost any hope of solving their problems on their own. Indeed, villainizing someone else so you can be the hero is a time-tested manipulation technique that will work as long as humans have wants and desires.

An equally common, but less discussed, means of hero manipulation is to find people who are committed to helping others and concoct a drama where their help can make a big difference. The manipulator then preys on the desire for good-natured souls to take heroic action and invest their money into a solution that never existed.

As these examples suggest, leveraging Karpman's hero concept is the tool of con artists, confidence men, and authoritarians. It can lead to some very dark outcomes in business, politics, and our personal relationships. Becoming the hero commits the other person to remaining a victim and keeps them powerless and in your debt. It makes them easy to manipulate to the point that they may do things out of gratitude to their hero that they will later regret. This places us back in the world of Don Corleone and the purposefully ambiguous "favor" he may or may not ever ask for.

Equally, becoming attached to the emotional and ethical satisfaction of playing the hero can make you vulnerable to others. Some of the biggest frauds in society disguise themselves as important social causes and charities. Sometimes, they are simply disguised as a friend who knows you can't say no because you need to play the hero's role.

All of which is to say, this is powerful black magic that is best avoided.

Escape the Triangle

If we aren't going to turn ourselves into heroes, then what can we do about all this drama? Once we recognize we're in the Drama Triangle, we face a fork in the road. We can take the dark path of manipulation, or we can follow the Tao and help guide the other person out of the triangle entirely.

According to Jim Dethmer, an executive coach and author of *The 15 Commitments of Conscious Leadership*, our aim should be to help people escape victim consciousness, a perspective that creates the illusion that life is happening *to* them and not *by* them. Defeating their villains only reinforces that victim consciousness. We want to break that paradigm entirely.[29]

We do this by finding the exit to drama through the aforementioned *co-creation*. In co-creation, we don't *save* the other person; we *partner* with them to develop solutions together.

This process begins the same way it would if you were seeking to become the hero. When you notice drama entering the conversation, you mindfully note which parties are filling the various corners of the triangle. Why do they feel like they're the victim? What part of their life feels victimized? Who is their villain? Is it you? Who is the hero they're looking for? Themselves? You? Someone else?

At the same time, you can inventory your own feelings. What emotions are you experiencing around this person? Are you feeling energized and heroic? Weak and victimized? Like you want to be purposefully contradictory and throw "truth bombs" like an antagonist or a villain?

Once you've mapped the roles in your mind, you can turn this introspection on the other person in the room and thus begin to understand the investor's internal operating system. In other words, you can develop a clear portrait of the personal or emotional needs they feel aren't being addressed. From there, you should empathize—perhaps with a gentle "I hear you"—before pivoting to a solution you co-create together.

Here's how it works in practice: I once had an investment opportunity that was attractive to a major client of mine. The client spent a lot of time evaluating the opportunity and determined it was a perfect fit for his program. The only problem was that I knew several of my other clients would also find the opportunity attractive, and I didn't want to exclude them. I was aware, therefore, that this major investor was going to create Scarcity or FOMO in the investment once everyone heard how much money he was prepared to invest.

Armed with this knowledge, I told my other clients there would probably not be enough room to accommodate everyone and formally launched the fundraising process. Many investors were understandably upset. I assured them that we would be fully transparent with our allocation process and decisions. To help ease everyone's disappointment, I reminded each investor that this was a catch-22 situation; the only reason I was able to offer the opportunity in the first place was because I had secured a large anchor investor.

Then the unthinkable happened. My anchor investor called to tell me that his company had installed a new CIO, and this new boss was going to nix the deal at the upcoming investment committee meeting. Normally, this investor was very reliable. But he had just met for the first time with his new boss, who was much more unpredictable and had no relationship with me or my firm.

I was in a real bind with no obvious good options. On the one hand, I could simply accept the situation and refuse to fight back. The deal would then collapse when he pulled out, as it would send a negative signal to the other investors who were relying on the anchor investor. On the other hand, I could practice the dark arts and try to shame my client into pushing the investment through. I could utilize the Drama Triangle and turn him into the villain in my story, manipulating him into an investment he wasn't comfortable or authorized to make. Equally, I could stoke the sense that his new boss was a villain who was going to blow up our relationship and thereby push my contact to find a way to move forward anyway. This would avoid the collateral damage that a last-minute veto would cause between our two organizations, but it would likely cause longer-term damage to our relationship, not to mention his relationship with his CIO and investment committee.

Instead, I took a third path. I recognized that my client was stuck in the Drama Triangle and that it was my duty to help him escape. I said, "I know you didn't want this to happen. I can see how much it's stressing you out, and we both know the consequences if your investment falls through. Rather than pressuring your new CIO to make the investment, perhaps we can have you make the full investment, and I will syndicate down your position shortly after closing? After all, we both knew that there were many other investors who, while much smaller, wanted to participate in the deal. This is a win-win for everyone. You believe strongly in the investment. Your CIO will likely be able to support the investment if it is smaller. My other investors will be thrilled to get more allocation to the deal. What do you think?"

The anchor investor said he was willing to do this under one condition: He wanted the right to be the lead investor in the next round of financing for this company. Even though his new CIO had nearly blown up the deal, I thought this was a great idea since it would give the CIO time to see the investment grow. Once the company proved its value as an investment, that newly impressed CIO would give the company access to a substantial source of future funding.

Thus, instead of building up the villainy of his new boss, I co-created a solution with my client (and now good friend) and executed a solution by which everyone came out ahead.

Moreover, this approach avoided the risk of a toxic relationship within the Karpman Drama Triangle and, as a bonus, still created a sense of Reciprocity, which increased the client's trust and decreased their fear. I had proven, after all, to be someone they could trust to be their partner.

Shooting the Messenger

In the fundraising world, Karpman's drama dynamic most often bears down on the person designated the *messenger*. Remember, the vast majority of institutional money is controlled by committees and decision-makers who live and die by approving the best investment ideas that people bring to them. Even the most successful fundraisers don't have direct access to these people. So, we are reduced to convincing others to get their organizations to say yes to our ideas. And that person, for lack of a better term, is a messenger.

Unfortunately, that's always been a dangerous position. In the ancient world, one of the worst jobs available was the imperial messenger. On most days, it was easy work. He went from the palace to some lavish estate with a missive concerning boring matters of economy or from one kingdom to another, sharing boring matters of state. But on the rare occasions when the messenger had to deliver bad news to powerful people, he found himself in a precarious position.

When an emperor or an aristocrat received upsetting news, their natural instinct was to indulge their anger and take it out on whoever ruined their mood. Such was the case with Tigranes II, king of Armenia, whose messengers were afraid to share news about the approach of Roman general Lucullus after the first messenger to mention it "had his head cut off for his pains."[30] Ouch.

Famously, the Spartans threw the Persian messenger who delivered King Darius's demand for their submission into a well. The Athenians responded similarly, throwing the Persian messengers into a gorge.[31] And in Shakespeare's *Antony and Cleopatra*, Cleopatra tells the messenger who has told her of Antony's marriage to another:

> Hence, horrible villain, or I'll spurn thine eyes
> Like balls before me! I'll unhair thy head![32]

These threats and acts of violence occurred despite being forbidden by any number of religious doctrines and legal statutes. Protection has been guaranteed to messengers for thousands of years—at least in theory. In fact, the expression "don't shoot the messenger" originated in ancient Greece. But such laws can prove ineffective against the default human reaction to particularly upsetting obstacles. When we receive bad news or are denied something we really want, we feel like victims, and the easiest thing to do is to transfer the role of the villain tormenting us from the responsible parties who are out of reach to the person right in front of us. There's no better way to stop feeling like a victim than to lop off a messenger's head for daring to tell you the Romans are on the way to topple your kingdom.

Luckily, investors are not in the habit of beheading the colleagues they disagree with. But that doesn't mean they have stopped indulging in that same *type* of retribution behavior.

For this reason, success in fundraising isn't always determined by convincing the person in the room. You can do everything right—build up their desire, reduce their fears, and create an indestructible argument that features *logos*, *ethos*, and *pathos*—and you can still end up with a no. Why? Often it's because the messenger isn't confident that your pitch will work on their boss.

One of the great truths of fundraising is that *every decision-maker is someone else's messenger.* This is particularly the case in a meritocracy, where the person in the room has a boss, who has a boss, who has a boss, and so on. In most corporate structures, even the CEO has to share the message of their decisions with the board and investors. If their audience is not receptive, they can lose their head—or rather, their job. Even in a tribal decision-making culture, the person in the room becomes a messenger to others in their tribe. And no one wants to deliver a bad message.

No matter what form it takes, being a messenger is a fearful position, and that fear produces drama. Recently, I had to tell one of my investors that we are not going to change our terms to accommodate his investment committee's request. He and I have been good friends for many years, and I know he wants to make an investment with my firm. However, he is afraid that his superiors are going to blame him for being an inadequate negotiator, or worse, get angry with him and shut the door on the investment.

And he's not just afraid; he's angry with me because he feels like I put him in this situation. After all, I could have just agreed to his committee's demands, and the stress would have been avoided. Or so he feels. In many ways, I am also just a messenger for my superiors.

Fortunately, as we have already seen, I have been here before. So, I've lost no sleep over this conflict. Unlike those unlucky ancient messengers, I know exactly how to deal with these situations. I'll start by giving my friend plenty of time to just be angry. I'll tell him to let me have it until he feels complete. After that, I will repeat back what he said to make sure he knows I "heard him." This confirmation will let him know that I understand. I get it. I know where he's coming from. I know he feels like the victim and, in this moment, I seem like the villain. This also serves as a check to see if he is truly done venting.

From there, I can turn the conversation away from anger and show him that he's got the roles wrong. He isn't a victim, and I'm not his enemy. In reality, we're partners, and if we work together, we can co-create a solution that works for both of us. I may have to go back to my team and find a compromise, but that's okay because I am not afraid to find a win-win. If I can convince him that we are on the same side, then he will not be afraid to deliver my message to his investment committee because he'll know that we are both determined to find common ground.

This isn't an easy feat to perform. It requires an understanding of the investor's psychology and an ability to compromise if necessary.

And to be clear, sometimes a compromise is not possible. But even in these situations, in my experience, it's more important to prevent the investor from getting swept up into victim consciousness, which often creates a righteousness that makes further dialogue nearly impossible. Therefore, even when a compromise can't be found, my aim is to find an exit to the Drama Triangle for all parties.

In the end, the Tao suggests that when confronted with drama, the best course of action is almost always to help lead others out by empowering them to create solutions or to challenge the validity of their own fears and concerns. It's not always about the persuasive techniques you bring to the game. Sometimes, it's about what makes for a stronger, healthier, and more durable relationship.

After all, people may shoot the messenger, but they don't shoot a friend helping them solve their problems.

Chapter 9

Persona Grata

As children, we learn behaviors that allow us to get what we need. Through a process called *mimetic modeling*, we observe our parents and other adults, we see how certain behaviors are received, and then we copy them ourselves. Using observation, trial, and error, we discover what behaviors work best in various scenarios. These behaviors eventually pool into "personas"—essentially character roles—that we experiment with, like trying on outfits.

If you think back, you can probably remember a time when you tried out being the class clown, the music snob, or the cynic. You might have had a period as the poet, the hard-nosed truth teller, or the ultra-reliable supportive friend.

This same persona play continues well after childhood and adolescence. It simply becomes more subtle. Though it can seem counterintuitive, none of us have a single personality. We all contain a multitude of personas we shift between depending on the circumstances before us. Our personality is on a continuum that we vacillate along from moment to moment.

Consider how we behave slightly differently with our parents than with friends. Likewise, our persona shifts when we feel fear, lust, or sadness. As our internal and external context changes, we might be more humorous, tender, sensitive, or stoic. We might clench our jaw and stand up straight, or let our shoulders droop and our gaze fall to the floor. We speak more firmly or softly. Our vocabulary changes. In each moment, we are playing a character, a version of ourselves.

For most people, these shifts are subconscious. When sad, a morose persona presents itself. In a business environment, the sober, logical persona peeks out. But when you're a fundraiser, there's immense value in bringing decisions about persona to a conscious level. This can allow you to *choose* the persona that best suits the needs of the other person in the room—increasing the connection between you and making persuasion more possible.

The Power of Persona Play

Remember, according to the Copernican theory of fundraising, the other person in the room is your sun, and everything you do must revolve around them. For this reason, you don't want to walk in and entrust your choice of persona entirely to your subconscious.

This is a somewhat subtle point. Our natural instinct is to see the person before us as sharing their full personality, but this is never the case. Instead, the other person is presenting a particular aspect of themselves, one they have likely refined over many years. This is the persona they put on when they are being asked for money.

The investor has expectations and preferences for how they want the other person to interact with this persona. If you get this wrong, you can end up with a firm *no* before you even get through the pitch. This is particularly tricky because your instinctive persona selection may prove inadequate for this specific interaction.

For instance, like many people, I naturally put on a self-deprecating persona in many situations. I do this in part because it's so effective. It puts people at ease. It invites intimacy and humor. Walking into the room, you might assume this is a smart persona to put on. After all, it can be charming, and most people like it. But self-deprecation with the wrong investor can undermine their confidence in you. Waving off your experience and credentials can lead the investor to wave them off as well.

To avoid such mistakes, we have to engage in *persona play*. According to psychologist and relationship expert Gay Hendricks, persona play can powerfully improve all of our relationships—and that includes our relationships with investors.[33]

Persona play allows us to consciously choose a persona instead of leaving it up to the desires and fears that usually determine our instinctive persona decision. We can't afford to be in that position in the room because we have to address the persona the investor is presenting. Their persona absolutely projects *their* needs—their fears, their desires—and we have to address those needs instead of our own.

They're projecting a need for us to know they are impressive or powerful. They're projecting a fear of being taken advantage of. They're projecting that they want us to think they like us because they need to feel liked and appreciated.

They need someone who laughs harder at their jokes. They need someone who takes charge and tells them everything is going to be okay. They need someone who will admire their brilliance.

If you understand their persona, you can accommodate it and make far more progress far more quickly.

Placing Bets

This is like a persona MMA match. As one fighter approaches, the other can read what style of fighting their opponent will use in their initial strike. With that information, they can choose a style that best counters the attack. That choice might be to match style for style, or it might be to use techniques that can absorb the attack before countering.

There's no single right decision in the fight. But understanding what is coming and what your options are allows you to place bets on what techniques will give you the best shot at winning.

This isn't just advice for the ring; it's also for the chessboard. In a great line from the movie *Searching for Bobby Fischer*, Laurence Fishburne's character, Vinnie, counsels the young chess prodigy, Josh Waitzkin: "Never play the board, always the man. You've gotta play the man playing the board. Play me. I'm your opponent; you have to beat me. Not the board. Beat me."[34]

Chess is equal parts strategy and placing bets on the persona of the person across the table from you. As Vinnie says, you're playing the player playing the board. How traditional are they? How adventurous? Are they the sort of player to go for a high-risk strategy, or do they stick to classic maneuvers?

Reading these persona qualities is as important as knowing how to recognize strategies like the Scotch Game or the Queen's Gambit.

The same is true in fundraising. If you want success in the room, you have to focus on the other person and place your bet on the best persona to match the one they are playing.

The Players

So, who are you playing against? According to journalist Will Storr, you are likely to encounter three types of players: those playing a *skills* game, those playing a *virtue* game, and those playing a *dominance* game.[35]

A *skills player* prioritizes demonstrating their expertise and prizes speaking to others who possess similarly impressive levels of expertise. Think of the professors who insist on being referred to as "Doctor" or the sci-fi pedants who will pull you up for slightly misremembering a scene in a *Star Wars* movie you saw years ago. What matters here is that they are experts, they show they're experts, and they expect you to be an expert. They also want to prove they're right about the subject—because they want to show they know the subject better than everyone else.

For the *virtue player*, what matters most is getting what they believe is morally or emotionally right. They aren't looking to debate what is *factually* right like the skills player. What's "right" isn't determined by breaking down the logic of the situation; it is a moral imperative. They want to change the world, and they need someone who wants to help them achieve that. To find virtue players, look no further than every group of activists you've ever heard of. Whether it's Second Amendment rights or veganism, the right path forward is clear to everyone in the group. What they want is an ally who can help them find ways of getting to their preferred result. They want to talk to people who want to be part of the team and bring in some fresh ideas.

A *dominance player*, by contrast, wants to win at all costs. They want you to know they are the top dog in this conversation, and they want to feel they have all the power. It's less about right and wrong or expertise than about being able to show they're king of the hill. Case in point: the CEO who's happy to sit back and let everyone else debate, just so long as they get to make the final call. Any pushback they receive is only acceptable coming from a subordinate improving the dominance player's decision.

These player personas all exist to varying degrees within each of us. And while I've given stereotypical examples—it's possible to be a virtue player CEO, a skills player activist, or a dominance player sci-fi fan—for the most part, most people will affect one or another of these players in the room.

You are trying to get something from them, so you have to let them set the rules, and then respond to the persona type they open with. To do that, you need a set of personas to choose from that match their opening move.

My Personas

To raise persona play to a conscious level, I find it helpful to name the personas I don in the room. You might choose to do the same or not, but for the purposes of this book, I think it will help to separate the characters I play when I encounter the various investor players I come up against.

Fortuitously, these players and personas also map onto Cialdini, providing us a vocabulary for the mixture of traits on display in each encounter.

Skills

The skills player lives largely in the world of *logos*. They love the craft behind their work and the ideas behind investment. They want to be around smart people, and winning for them is winning a contest of ideas with peers who can appreciate their genius.

When playing opposite a skills player, you don't want to use a persona that relies heavily on Cialdini's Liking principle. Charm can work against you because it may suggest you lack a certain seriousness and depth. Instead, you want a persona that brings out Authority, Consensus, and Consistency. The skills investor wants an erudite professor. They want you to bring out your inner academic and prepare for an old-fashioned debate.

"Professor Kim"

This is one of the most common personas I bring into the room because, in my world, the majority of investors are skills players. Generally speaking, they have to be hyper-intelligent experts who enjoy getting into the details of a deal. That's the only way to consistently make a profit as a professional investor playing in the private or public markets. When considering a new deal, they are looking to discuss the prospect with someone as serious and thoughtful as they are themselves.

That's when I invite "Professor Kim" to the table. This version of my persona is all *logos*. I've done the research. I've studied the facts. I have the experience. This is the persona with all the details at hand—a generous teacher who is ready to answer any question in as much detail as they could possibly want.

As a teacher, Professor Kim is also looking to bring out the best qualities in his intellectual colleague. He wants to help the skills player be right and have all the facts to prove their rightness.

He's not entirely without charm. After all, a great professor brings a certain charisma to their subject. But he's concise, dry, and pithy. All his charm goes to elucidating the ideas at hand.

Virtue

The virtue investor is largely interested in *ethos*. They have to feel the topic at hand is important to some larger goal or bigger purpose. This investment may make them money, but more importantly, it has to *mean something*. That meaning can vary widely, but it comes back to making the world a better place in some way that the investor feels deeply about.

A virtue player needs the persona on the other side of the room to zero in on their *ethos* goals and offer them Consistency in their approach to achieve those goals as well as Authority on the subject to convince them that this improvement can happen. They also need a generous serving of personal connection to help the medicine go down.

However, the main component of this persona is Reciprocity. In particular, the virtue investor needs to know that if they put something in, they'll get something back in the form of an improvement that aligns with their values.

"Coach Kim"

The virtue player is looking for a coach. They want someone who will be transparent and tell them what they have to give in order to get what they want for the world.

"What are you willing to give up to make this happen? Let's name it and make it happen!"

That's where "Coach Kim" comes in. Coach Kim is willing to tell them that there will be pain if they want to achieve that gain. He wants to know the goal so they can both reckon with what it takes to get there. He's willing to make the tough calls to ensure that goal is achieved.

Coach Kim is this investor's virtue personal trainer, helping them get their goals in shape.

"You told me these are your goals," he might tell a virtue investor. "This is what you need to do to get there."

At the same time, he relies on a large dose of *pathos*-fueled Liking for inspiration. He shares their goals, and he likes them personally for having those goals. Because Coach Kim shares their vision and personal Liking, he wants them to do this valuable thing together.

Dominance

I have saved dominance for last because it is the most complicated player type to respond to. Skills and virtue players are fairly straightforward. On a very basic level, you are simply responding with heavily *logos-* or *ethos*-influenced personas, meeting like for like.

But that often isn't so easy with *pathos*-infused dominance players. They want to *feel* like they're in charge, and trying to meet dominance with dominance is a high-risk strategy likely to spiral into the Drama Triangle. Instead, you usually want to meet that aggressive persona with one that can absorb the emotional energy coming at you and flip it into something more productive. And there are several different techniques you can employ to do that.

"THE SMOOTH OPERATOR"

Your first option is the charm offensive known as the "Smooth Operator." Pick a Hollywood debonair, charismatic individual and channel their energy into your persona.

For me, I choose slick, handsome, easygoing good guy Cary Grant, whom you film lovers probably fell in love with in *His Girl Friday, The Philadelphia Story, Bringing Up Baby,* or any one of the dozens of charming performances he gave over his career. But if you'd rather, you could go with Hugh Grant, George Clooney, Julia Roberts, or Jennifer Aniston.

The main point is that each of these individuals is intelligent, kind, charming, and eager to please without ever coming across as desperate or weak. You can imagine any of them responding to an aggressive, self-important individual with a disarming grin, a little gentle humor, and a classy turn of phrase that reframes the subject at hand.

More importantly, while all of the examples above are undeniably physically attractive, sexuality doesn't play a part in this persona. Instead, this is the role of the professional charmer. And it works very well with dominance players because the Smooth Operator doesn't mind if the other person gets to claim the win. They're happy to delicately suggest a different course and let the other person take the credit.

This is a persona that is dripping with Liking and adds a bit of Reciprocity on top.

"You're coming at me hard," the Smooth Operator might say with a disarming grin. "I get it. And I can get what you want. But I'm going to need something from you to make sure it happens."

When things get bogged down a bit, I might give a little laugh, and throw in some Consistency, reminding them that every time we go down a particular road they're demanding we follow, it delays us, and I want them to get what they want. I want them to win. And since they like me, they trust me.

After all, as we know already, charm is really just a form of Liking. It tells the other player that "I like them, and I am like them," and because of my charm, they like me too. That lowers their defensiveness and flips their aggressiveness into a desire for partnership. I've given away the right to call this my win, so we're on the same side.

And as a bonus, because of this Liking, the dominance player now often desires *my* approval. They like me, and they want to be sure I like them—giving me more power in the relationship.

"The Maître d'"

There's a similar persona available for particularly needy dominance players. These investors attempt to prove their dominance by constantly demanding your attention and effort.

For these players, I put on the restaurant "Maître d'" persona. I let them know they're my priority customer. I'm happy to do whatever small thing I can to make their wait more comfortable. But I can't seat them until the table is ready. I'd love to, but it's beyond my power.

I give them the equivalent of a nice glass of wine and a seat at the bar. I check on them regularly and refill their glass. I commit to immediately telling them when circumstances change. But until then, I set firm boundaries. The Maître d' is basically the Smooth Operator persona with the slightest dash of Authority—just enough to show that I have some power here without inciting a conflict over dominance.

"John Draper"

I've mentioned that matching dominance against dominance is a high-risk play. But that doesn't mean it's always the wrong choice. There are times when the *easiest* way to win a fight is not the most *sophisticated*. Sometimes, the simplest path to victory is to overpower the opponent and throw them to the ground.

That's where someone like Don Draper comes in. He's the confident, no-nonsense, truth-telling marketer who is the protagonist of the show *Mad Men*. Don has a number of negative character traits that affect his personal life, but in the ad-pitch room, he's always the one willing to tell everyone the unvarnished truth—even when they don't want to hear it. They can decide what to do with that truth. Don doesn't care. When I shift into this persona, I think of myself as "John Draper."

"You can't afford to be happy?" John Draper might tell an investor. "Okay, nice to know that."

There's a famous scene in *Mad Men* in which Draper exhibits this full-throttle Authority attitude. He's sharing an elevator with Ginsberg, a talented but green marketer on his team who is upset with him. Ginsberg says, "I feel bad for you," trying to inflict the same sting of rejection Ginsberg felt after Draper undermined him in front of a client.

Draper, though, doesn't miss a beat. "I don't think about you at all," he says, then walks out of the elevator without a glance at the stunned underling.[36]

That's the attitude you can bring to the dominance player investor. "Take it or leave it. It's no skin off my back."

Importantly, while this persona maxes out Authority, it also leverages Liking. There's almost always a charm to Draper's condescension, especially when he deftly puts clients in their place. It's why a successful show could be built around him. We like him. We're rooting for him, even as we often shake our heads at his behavior. He's cold, cutting, but still incredibly likable. Ginsberg was trying to hurt his feelings because, deep down, he wants Draper's approval.

This is a hard balance to find, and it's possible only when you have the experience and expertise to back it up. You can't say you don't care about the investor's decision if you really *do* care whether they say yes or no. For that reason, you should not even consider this persona unless you are in a position to prove your dominance.

Essentially, don't *play* Goliath until you *are* a Goliath. Don Draper could get away with it because he was a master ad man. He was highly respected and brilliant, and everyone knew it. You don't have to be a thirty-year fundraising veteran to use this persona, but you have to be in a fairly powerful position.

Even when you are in that position, I still recommend saving this persona for rare occasions. There are usually better, more elegant ways to get what you want—ways that are more likely to strengthen your relationship with the investor. This is simply a good option to keep in your back pocket for the times when nothing else will work.

The Meta-Persona

The above persona postures work in a vacuum with a single investor who maintains a consistent persona throughout your interaction. Of course, when you're in the room, you'll find it is nothing like a vacuum. Investors often have partners who exhibit different personas. And a single investor may switch from a dominance to a virtue player over the course of a single meeting.

To handle all these complexities, there's value in relying on a meta-persona. A *meta-persona* is an accumulation of all the various personas you may employ in the room. It's likely similar to the default state you have when meeting a new person—a persona that leaves all your major options open. It's a starting point from which you can easily transition between personas as necessary.

Your meta-persona should be nonthreatening to ease tension with a dominance player, exhibit intelligence and expertise that would impress a skills player, and easily talk about the value of the work in a way that aligns with the needs of a virtue player.

For me, this meta-persona is "Kimmer." The moniker itself is extremely nonthreatening. It sounds almost like a "bro" nickname I picked up in a fraternity. Kimmer is a friendly and amusing persona, but he's also hyper-competent and quick to dive into the important figures behind a potential investment. Kimmer is passionate about the causes behind the investment. He's happy to explain why he cares and what the fund can do about these issues in as much detail as a virtue or skills player requires.

It's very easy for me to pivot from Kimmer to Professor Kim, Coach Kim, or the Smooth Operator, since all of them enter the room when I do. It's a seamless shift that allows me to flow with the conversation.

If you can establish and refine this kind of meta-persona, you'll be able to shift between personas in real time, depending on whom you're addressing and their needs in the moment.

Personas Are Personal

This is not an exhaustive list of my personas or even of the personas that I bring into the room. There are times when I bring a more childlike, innocent persona—one stripped completely of Authority that looks at a dominance player with the reverence I'd normally reserve for a parental figure. There's also a "Mr. Dad" persona that leverages the opposite impulses, gently and paternally guiding an uncertain investor toward the wise answer only I can see clearly.

What unites these personas is that they are natural extensions of myself. Personas are not meant to be characters you invent whole cloth. To try to "play" a persona that is outside your natural personality risks coming across as completely fake to the investor—because it is, in fact, a completely fake persona. Remember, we are working in the realm of *what is*. We aren't creating fiction; we're molding a particular perception of reality.

You have a natural range of ways to engage with the world, and you want to work with the nuances that exist within that spectrum. If you are not naturally funny, don't try to assume a funny persona.

For this reason, I recommend doing a mindful inventory of all the various ways you interact with people in your life. If you want to name these personas, as I have, that can be worthwhile because it can make them easier to call on. However, even just being aware of how you behave in various situations and knowing you have the ability to shift personas consciously can allow you to recognize what type of behavior you're demonstrating in the room and when to adjust it.

Choosing a Persona

With a whole closetful of personas you can use on demand, you can prepare for the room by making an educated guess about which persona to employ before walking in. For instance, as I write this, I'm meeting later today with a young woman who will be investing in one of my funds. My assumption is that she's probably sick of men trying to charm her. She's likely also sick of people undervaluing her experience and intelligence.

So, I'm going to put on the Professor Kim persona before we even shake hands. Throughout the whole meeting, I will be all about the facts of the fund. Where I might normally focus on asking questions to get to know her more closely, I'm going to stick with being strictly professional. After that, I have a meeting with an entrepreneurial CEO whom

I know quite well. He loves approval and close friendships, so I'll bring the Kimmer persona into that meeting and maybe shift into the Smooth Operator if I need to kick the charm up a notch.

You won't be certain if your assumptions are correct until you've settled into a conversation with an investor. For example, some people take great pride in how they look, and they want others to notice. There's a spectrum of flirtation that exists across our experiences, and while it would always be inappropriate to dial that number up above a three out of ten in a business setting, some investors—both men and women—want you to move above a one. They want you to charm them; they want to know you've noticed how they look. In that kind of situation, I might need to bring a little Smooth Operator or even John Draper into the conversation.

Of course, there are times when a potential investor—even someone you know quite well—will show up in a completely different mood, and therefore persona, than you expected. For example, my CEO friend may be in a less jovial mood today. He might be under pressure from his board. He might need solid answers now. If I pick up on that early in the meeting, I know I'll need to switch into Professor Kim mode with him, skipping the jokes and banter and diving soberly into the numbers.

For this reason, I tend to start each meeting with a little small talk. A few minutes spent discussing life can build rapport and give you a sense of the other person in the room—both who they are and who they are *today*. This is valuable even if you discover it slightly annoys the investor. After all, annoyance may signal a dominance player who wants to be in control of the meeting. That is very useful information to have.

As the conversation continues, keep an eye out for a shift in persona from the other person in the room. You can usually see when someone's persona changes if you're paying attention. You can read their emotional state from their body language or tone of voice. Reading this effectively allows you to respond to their desires and fears through a corresponding shift in your own persona.

It's even possible to break through persona play dynamics entirely by calling them out directly. I'll sometimes point out that I recognize the persona in front of me and let the investor know that I understand why they are putting it on. For example, if I notice them slip into a skeptical dominance persona halfway through our conversation, I might say:

> I can't convince you of this in one conversation, but I'd love to have another conversation to see if I could get you from "probably no" to "probably yes." I understand I can never get you to 100 percent, but I'd love a chance to shift you to 80 percent. We both know those perfect investments are rare, and we have to take chances. All I'm asking is for an opportunity to show you this is worth that chance.

If you're thinking this all feels a bit overwhelming, you are absolutely right. And I want to be clear that you don't have to take persona play this far. Working on persona at an elite level is not for everyone, but the more conscious you are of the way you communicate and behave in the room, the more you can influence the direction the conversation takes, creating more opportunities for success.

Chapter 10

The Audition

When you see him on-screen now, it's hard to imagine anyone playing Thor but Chris Hemsworth. He's tall, strong, beautiful, funny, and imperious when he wants to be. He's perfect for the role. He *is* Thor.

But he very nearly wasn't. At his first audition, he was dismissed out of hand. According to the Norse god himself, his audition "sucked." In fact, it wasn't until his younger brother, Liam, caught the attention of casting directors months later that Chris got a second shot and finally showed everyone he was born to play the role. By then, he had more experience, and he came in with a "different attitude."[37]

That attitude change was key. To really inhabit a character, an actor has to look the part and feel the part at the same time. It wasn't until Hemsworth combined the two that he could convince the casting directors that they had their Thor.

Hemsworth isn't the only one to beat the odds and ace a superhero audition. One of the most famous true stories of a successful movie audition is that of Hugh Jackman for the role of Wolverine in the *X-Men* franchise.

In the late 1990s, Jackman was relatively unknown outside of Australia and had primarily worked in theater and television. When casting began for the first *X-Men* film (which was released in 2000), another actor was set to portray Wolverine. However, due to scheduling conflicts, Jackman was called in for a last-minute audition.

At the time, Jackman seemed better suited for a Rodgers and Hammerstein musical than a Marvel action movie. Yet during his audition, he famously brought a dark and raw energy to the character, showcasing Wolverine's fierce and brooding nature. Director Bryan Singer was impressed not only by Jackman's acting but also by his ability to embody the tough, complex persona of Wolverine.

Despite concerns about his physical appearance—at six-foot-two, he was far taller than the five-foot-three character in the comic books—Jackman's passion and talent won over the casting team. He ultimately got the part, and his portrayal of Wolverine became iconic. As of this writing, he holds the record for an actor playing the same superhero character the longest, having portrayed Wolverine for nearly twenty-five years across eleven on-screen appearances (and counting!). With that one audition, he set himself on course to go from a relatively unknown actor to a global superstar.

The Craft

Fundraising and acting have a lot in common. They both require a great deal of psychological insight, skill, and practice—all in an effort to perform for an audience. Further, viewing fundraising through the lens of acting allows us to better understand our time in the room.

Too often, novice fundraisers see it as an *interview* of the sort we all do when job hunting. In reality, it is an *audition*. Like an actor standing in front of a casting director, you will be judged on far more than your résumé and how well you answer a few questions. Indeed, everything about your *performance* will be under inspection.

I use the word "performance" deliberately because, make no mistake, fundraising is a performance. How you dress, how you sound, the persona you employ when walking in, your tone when you answer objections—all the nuances of performance make all the difference when you are sitting across from investors.

Your ability to master the craft of auditioning will go a long way toward determining how an investor views what you're selling. And that will determine how likely they are to ultimately say yes. A great audition can sell a mediocre product, and a poor audition can sink an otherwise excellent opportunity.

You can hand Meryl Streep or Robert De Niro a middling script, and they can turn it into something memorable. An overall forgettable movie like *Taken* becomes a sensation because Liam Neeson is so electric in the role. And it's hard to imagine anyone else playing Wolverine or P. T. Barnum in *The Greatest Showman* but Hugh Jackman.

At that same time, we've all seen potentially good movies that were let down by bad acting—be it terrible accents, awkward line delivery, or inexplicable emotions. It doesn't matter how strong the script or direction is on such projects; they ultimately become either unwatchable or a joke.

We can also think of movies that even great actors couldn't save. There was no world where even Al Pacino could save *Jack and Jill*. The cast of the 2019 film adaptation of *Cats* included Judi Dench, Ian McKellen, and Jennifer Hudson, yet most people consider it as appealing as a hairball. In other words, a movie doesn't *just* come down to the talent of the actors.

In the same way, there has to be *something of value* in what you're selling. Assuming that is the case, though, with the Tao's theory of mind and some choice performance decisions, you can turn an average proposition into an exceptional pitch.

First Impressions Matter

Ask any actor, and they'll tell you that first impressions matter. In an audition, you want to show immediately that you fit the physical, emotional, and philosophical expectations of the other person in the room. In both acting and fundraising, your main concern is the *other person's* experience. Whether you're an actor in front of a casting director or a fundraiser in front of an investor, your aim is not to be *yourself.* Your job in that moment is to be *what they need you to be.*

An audition is not about expressing yourself; it's about playing to the expectations of the person who has the power to make the big decision. Acting is an art form that involves self-expression, but to express a character creatively, an actor must first impress the casting director. Otherwise, there's no part to play.

When inhabiting the role that meets the investor's expectations, don't discount the subtle things. We are pre-programmed with prejudices, assumptions, biases, and expectations for people who fill various roles in our lives. We have a picture in our mind of what a firefighter looks like and how they act, or how a CEO should comport themselves as they walk into a boardroom.

When I meet a personal trainer, I expect them to be fit. I expect a yoga trainer to be slim and flexible. I expect a philosophy professor to be thoughtful and perhaps somewhat aloof. If they're wearing a tweed jacket, all the better. There are many trainers, yoga instructors, and professors who don't fit those stereotypes, but it's more difficult for them to prove themselves to the majority of people who expect them to "look the part."

They must prove their expertise, as it isn't immediately apparent. Sometimes, they never get that chance. I may not even meet with an out-of-shape trainer or offer to sit down with a chatty, superficial professor.

If you look the part, sound the part, and feel the part, you are making your job much easier from the first moment you walk into the room. If you present the right body language and speak with the right tone, you increase trust and decrease fear in the other person in the room. You predispose them to give you the role.

Tailor Yourself to Your Audience

I was just in Asia visiting a number of extremely important investors, and in one meeting in particular, I blew it. The chairman for one firm was late to our meeting. When he walked in, I suggested I get him up to speed with our progress. Only afterward did I realize what a faux pas that was. In the culture I was visiting, the meeting shouldn't have even started without the chairman. Recounting our progress—normally a sign of politeness and deference—was likely a slight insult.

Perhaps because of that mistake, the process didn't advance beyond that first meeting. I failed the audition.

When you're walking into an audition, you have to be hyper-aware of the expectations being placed upon you. The way you conduct a meeting in California is different from how you conduct it in Michigan. In Wisconsin, be prepared to talk about the Packers. On Wall Street, no one wants to break the ice with talk about the Jets. Meetings in Texas are much more relationship-focused than they are on the East Coast, and they're much more informal on the West Coast than the East.

This isn't just about vibes and small talk, either. Don't underestimate the power of your uniform and what it communicates about you to the investor. There's a reason police officers, pilots, and doctors all have uniforms. They don't wear them because the outfits are comfortable or particularly functional (although they are). A uniform immediately confers a certain Authority—a sense that you know what you're doing. You belong to a certain club, and people should trust you as a representative of that club. This is almost putting us back into persona play, letting your clothes announce the role you are going to play.

Of course, a fundraiser doesn't technically have a uniform, but in practice, certain types of investors and fundraisers tend to share a similar wardrobe. If you're raising money on Wall Street from institutional investors, you better walk into the room in a suit or a dress and blazer. Out West, that would look far too stuffy. Instead, you probably want to go business casual. And if you're working in venture capital, you want to go even more casual than that. Venture capitalists tend to wear the uniform of jeans and a nice shirt with no tie. If you're raising money for a VC firm, that's how you want to show up, even if everyone else in the room is in a three-piece suit. Otherwise, you don't fit their expectations.

You always want to present yourself as successful in the world you represent. If you're raising money for a hip restaurant, you want to look hip, perhaps even a bit disheveled. If you're opening a dive bar, you want to have a blue-collar air about you. Showing up too polished in these cases suggests you don't inhabit the role expected of you.

There is room here to be a contrarian. You can be the only VC fundraiser who always dresses to the nines. You can walk into an investment bank in ripped jeans and a white T-shirt, and they may assume you are some kind of quirky genius. It's a higher-risk proposition, but you can surprise their expectations and engage the investor that way.

But even then, you are playing with expectations, not ignoring them. In my experience, you should look either exactly like what they expect or exactly the opposite of it. Ignoring expectations risks signaling that you don't belong at all.

Entering with the Right Attitude

Auditioning is a nerve-racking business. You stand in front of a tough room and offer yourself up to judgment. That isn't easy for most people, but you can't allow your nerves to get the best of you.

Those nerves are a fear response, triggered because this event feels on some level like a threat to your safety. Of course, your physical safety isn't in danger, but your ego certainly is. And by now, we know what that can trigger: the hero/villain/victim Drama Triangle.

It's easy to enter the room with a victim-sized chip on your shoulder. It isn't fair that you have to audition like this. Why do they have most of the power? Why do you have to go through all this just to get rejected? Why can't they see how good this product is without you having to jump through all these hoops?

If you walk into the room with a victim persona in place, you immediately open up that Drama Triangle for the investor as well. And if you've already removed your own power from the situation by making yourself a victim, you are likely to become the villain, wasting the victim investor's time.

Even if you avoid the Drama Triangle, entering with too much fear can only reduce your effectiveness. Imagine a salesperson trying to sell you on their company while their hands shake, they turn pale, and they keep wiping their brow. Do you trust that person or their company? Why should you? The person in front of you doesn't seem to believe what they're saying! That terrible first impression immediately puts the fundraiser into a deep hole he or she may never climb out of.

To reduce this fear response, you should remind yourself that there is no actual threat here. The audition may feel like a threatening situation, but it is not one. It's an act, a bit of play. Nothing terrible will happen to you in the room.

You can further reduce fear through the simple act of preparation. Every actor learns their script, and every fundraiser should know their product inside and out. This is where the Tao of Fundraising can be a further help. The Tao's theory of mind provides an extra layer of training—like studying acting at Juilliard and coming to an audition with a whole host of Meisner and Stanislavsky techniques.

At the same time, you can transform the role of the investor from villain to partner simply by adjusting your own expectations. Actor Kerry Washington once spoke of casting directors as fellow artists: "They are a scene partner, an audience member; they are in your corner."[38] Of course, we can assume that not every casting director behaves like that. Some will undoubtedly be impatient—even rude. But approaching them first as a partner can elevate the relationship and reduce your fears.

The same is true of the investor. At root, most investors are not seeking to humiliate you. Most don't even want to reject you. They want to find that person and that investment that their boss or client has asked them to find. They want you to be the person who can get them to yes. Approach them from that position of mutual interest, and you can remove the risk of dwelling on your own victimhood.

Authenticity and Effort in Every Pitch

Learning the art of acting just so you can raise capital may feel a bit overwhelming. The good news, though, is that you don't have to be flawless in the audition; you just have to be *memorable*. The best actors—Streep, De Niro, Pacino—present characters that are relatable. They don't hide the flaws; they place them in a context. A flawless character is impossible to relate to. We're suspicious of them. We think they're hiding something. And the same is true in the room.

When an interviewer asks what your biggest weakness is, the worst answer is one that pretends there are no weaknesses at all. Pretending there is no downside to your product or that you are endlessly accommodating without any boundaries only makes an investor doubt more. It makes them think: *What's the catch?*

Instead, like an actor, your aim should be authenticity. In fundraising, you have to be willing to show that you and your pitch aren't perfect. There are risks. You can express a certain amount of doubt. And you can offer your best potential solutions.

This is no excuse, though, to give less than your best to every audition. You want to leave every investor saying, "That's the best fundraiser I've ever seen!" This is precisely what I tell my team. If they are going to make a presentation to their colleagues within the firm, they shouldn't do the minimum required to complete the task. Instead, they should aim to make it the best presentation the firm has ever seen—because this is their chance to show their peers how good they are at making presentations. And a great audition will give everyone the confidence that they are the right people to represent the firm to the outside world. They should always leave the presentation with everyone in the room saying, "I'm glad you are here."

Be the best model of what fundraising looks like—even when you know you aren't getting to yes. Because if you don't audition that way, when failure happens, you will always question whether it was *you* that cost you the deal.

Giving less than everything is never excusable. Even a pitch that is clearly heading toward rejection has value. That time in the room is an opportunity to practice your craft. It's an opportunity to apply the tactics and mind-sets we've explored in this book. A fundraiser on course for a decline from an investor can still practice reducing fear through Cialdini's techniques and practice increasing desire through the *logos*, *ethos*, and *pathos* framework. They can still recognize and practice escaping the Drama Triangle. They can practice trying on various personas.

Every Audition Has Potential

You never know where an audition can lead. Hemsworth didn't get Thor on his first audition. He needed a few more rounds of practice before he was ready to blow the casting team away. A no can unexpectedly flip to a yes, but that's only possible if you keep chasing that yes to the very end.

I've seen people throw away opportunities to practice and potentially miss out on future opportunities. Just last week, a prestigious economics professor asked for a meeting with me. As he sat down, I told him up front that I was not on the investment side of my company. It was important he understood I couldn't connect him to any funding. I also said I was busy on a few fundraising projects myself and may get called away, but that my intention was to give him a full hearing and offer any feedback I could.

After this preamble, I watched his shoulders sink. Though he'd been fully warned about this ahead of time, the facts seemed to annoy him. He rushed through his presentation and got out of my office as quickly as possible.

Now, all that I had told him was true, but if he had blown me away, I could have gotten him into some important rooms with people who *could* fund him. He could have used me as a reference as he connected with investors—"I know Kimmer was impressed by this." Instead, he left me with a bad impression and earned a bad reference. No new open doors, and potentially a few closed ones.

It was a poor audition, and a costly one.

PART THREE

A Lifelong Practice

Chapter 11

Ego Deprivation

There are those who can sell anything, no matter how much real value is in the product. Some of these individuals are worshiped in the pantheon of salespeople (Dale Carnegie, Zig Ziglar), while others are seen as villains (Bernie Madoff, Charles Ponzi).

The difference between them is not so much their skill or technique as how they choose to pursue their art. Ultimately, the tools of the Tao can do great good or great harm, depending on the hands using them.

As we enter the third and final part of this book, my aim is to convince you to listen to your conscience, to use all that we have learned to find the value in whatever you're selling and pursue this practice with integrity.

To achieve this, we must embark on a journey of embodying the Tao throughout our lives. That journey starts with learning to sublimate our own interests, not just for the sake of the other person in the room, but in the name of the product we are selling.

Selling with Authenticity

The key to every sale is authenticity. This is far easier when you are the Principal versus the Agent. The Principal is the person who will use the money raised to bring the product to market successfully. It's the person who will run the new restaurant or the CEO heading up new research and development. Almost always, the Principal genuinely believes in their product. They would gladly sell it to their family members. That's why they're in this position.

But it's a little different if you want to harness the Tao to pursue fundraising as a career. In that case, you will be an Agent working on some sort of commission-like structure, selling products to investors, not necessarily because you believe in them but because you are paid to do it.

An Agent doesn't really have any skin in the game. They only care about the initial sale. Whatever happens afterward doesn't really affect them. This sometimes makes it harder for the fundraiser to develop an authentic interest in whatever product or organization they are representing.

Let me state very directly that a lack of authentic interest is perfectly fine in fundraising. There is so much written by people who espouse the notion that you have to believe in something passionately to sell it. If you don't, these authors argue, it's not worth it, and you'll lack sufficient motivation to close the deal. That is far too idealistic for me.

Consider the legal field. The best attorneys wage verbal combat in the courtroom, representing people whom they may or may not believe are innocent. In fact, they may even be sympathetic to their opponents. But the goal is to represent their client's side of the case to the best of their ability. A lawyer's ethical responsibility is to ensure that their client receives fair and zealous representation. They don't have to believe their clients are innocent or even good people.

The same principle applies when selling a product you aren't enthusiastic about. It is not unethical. It's practical, as long as there is some actual value in the product. The only time fundraising strays into unethical territory is if you believe the product is a certain failure or that your client is perpetrating some kind of scam. Otherwise, you are just selling an ordinary product—and the world is full of profitable, yet staggeringly ordinary, products.

If such products prove to be not just ordinary but mediocre or subpar, the market will figure that out eventually. In chapter 3, I mentioned that legendary ad man Jerry Della Femina once told me, "The only thing great marketing does for a bad product is put that product out of business faster." I've seen that maxim proven time and time again throughout my career. So, if you still struggle with the notion of raising funds for a product you aren't personally passionate about, you can take some comfort in knowing there is a sort of *karmic justice* in the end for many of those who build their business around a bad product.

However, many of the products fundraisers sell aren't bad; they just aren't exceptional. There are whole Fortune

100 companies dedicated to developing and selling the ordinary products that make the world go round—Procter & Gamble, Johnson & Johnson, and PepsiCo, just to name a few. There's nothing deeply interesting about any of their products. I don't mean to be dismissive of these successful businesses, but their products aren't particularly differentiated.

If you're going to pursue fundraising as a career, undifferentiated products or firms are precisely what you will represent most of the time—at least at first. These are the products where a fundraiser really makes their career. After all, no one needs a salesperson or a fundraiser for a product or investment idea that sells itself. In fact, there's a direct correlation between the increasing commoditization of a product or investment idea and the increasing need for marketing and sales.

That's where you come in, and the puzzle is figuring out how to sell what doesn't naturally sell itself.

Selling in the Right Frame of Mind

When you look at the rules of sales, the easiest way to develop a pitch is to think about why you would invest in a product or investment yourself. This is an obvious, well-known, and frequently taught rule. It is also tragically misguided and far too egocentric. This approach prioritizes your desire to be logically, emotionally, and ethically aligned with the potential opportunity. But there is one rather big problem with this approach: You are neither the buyer nor the investor.

As the Copernican theory states, your job is to put the *other person*—the investor—at the center of your sales pitch. You must figure out what makes this product special from *their* point of view, not from yours. Don't ask yourself, *Why would I want to put my own money into this?* Instead, you might ask, *What about this product would make my parents want to put their money—maybe even their life savings—into it?*

By removing yourself from the center of the equation, you distance yourself from your core interest in making money for yourself and give yourself higher stakes—allowing you to speak from a place of genuine conviction.

In considering this hypothetical, you don't have to assume away your concerns. The idea of taking money from loved ones might make you fearful. Obviously, no deal is foolproof and guaranteed. It would still be possible to lose money despite your best efforts. Those loved ones may not actually be in a position to invest, particularly in a high-risk scenario, but you have to believe in the reasons why they *might* invest.

The point here is that you need to come from a place of genuinely wanting to do well by the other person in the room. You aren't indifferent to them. You want to make *them* money. You want them to feel good about this investment. You have a *logos* or logical reason why the investment should work. You have an *ethos* or ethical belief in serving the other person's interests. And there's a *pathos* or emotional connection because you actually care.

In short, you understand the "specialness" of the product from their perspective.

Finding Specialness

Where do you find the specialness at the root of your product that unlocks these motivations?

Usually, it is tied to one of two pillars of success in the capitalist system. Remember, *capital*-ism is a system built on the belief that *capital* should flow to the best idea. The best idea usually addresses one of two issues:

- **Mispricing/Efficiency Gap**: The price or margin is irrationally high on an existing product or service. You can sell it for less, often by increasing efficiency in development or logistics.
- **New Opportunity**: There's something that society deems valuable that it does not yet have, and you can provide it.

In either case, addressing these concerns can be enduring or short-term. Some products are meant to make a quick buck—either by collapsing the pricing gap or filling a temporary opportunity. These products are more like trades than true investments. The turnaround is expected to be quick and unrepeatable. Many apps and games are like this. You'll release it, make some money, and then move on to the next thing. Investing in a particular movie works the same way. You'll see revenue from the theatrical run, from video on demand rental fees, and from the initial run on a streaming platform. While there is some longer-term revenue, those early revenue opportunities are where most of the return will come from, and, ideally, they add up to a nice onetime profit for all involved.

During the COVID-19 pandemic, the first companies who were able to sell masks and hand sanitizer at scale made a fortune.[39] That scenario was not an enduring one, but it was a profitable trade for investors.

Other products are meant to address a long-term demand. These hold enduring value for society. The iPhone is a great example. Apple's device led the way in the smartphone revolution by addressing a huge societal need to put mobile computing and the internet into our hands. The sheer dollars in the smartphone ecosystem suggest that society places huge value on being connected online and to each other electronically. There's no sign it will change in the near future. Likewise, Amazon's incredible ability to deliver a multitude of goods and services with unprecedented efficiency has no end in sight. Its pricing and logistical adjustments will continue to create value for consumers and investors for many years to come.

Of course, the natural enemy of endurance is innovation. BlackBerry had a product they felt was enduring, but they failed to innovate quickly enough to keep up with the iPhone or Android. There was a moment when the BlackBerry was very "special," as it served an important need for consumers and businesses, but the company simply couldn't keep up with the rapid pace of change.

Such eventualities are beyond the scope of your job as a fundraiser. You aren't responsible for determining if a company's leadership has the capability to continue to innovate or not. Your job is to make the best case for why the opportunity is *special*—not necessarily that it's *perfect*.

Expect Failure

Even if you have a special product you truly believe in, and align your entire mindset around the product and other people in the room, I guarantee you will still fail—often.

In fundraising, you may eventually achieve a 10 percent win record. You might even get to 20 percent—if you're really good. But even then, 80 percent of the time, you are going to walk out of the room after hearing a firm no.

As in any competitive sport, sometimes you just get beat. You prepare, train, and compete to win. But even then, even when you're the best, you are eventually going to lose. If you allow your ego to take this personally, you won't last. You simply have to come to terms with this reality. If you don't, you'll lose motivation and potentially give up completely.

The difference between sports competitions and fundraising is that, in sports, there is a measurable objective that lets you know if you are winning or losing. In fundraising, you can be losing and not have any clue. You can get meeting after meeting, moving farther and farther up the ladder of approvals and buy-in, only to discover the answer was always going to be no. Spending so much time and energy on a pitch that was doomed from the start can feel like a waste. And that can lead to some disastrous behavior. Sometimes, competitive people get locked into an egoic battle with the investor and start scoring against themselves without even knowing it. The sales pitch turns into an argument. The fundraiser will raise their voice. Fight-or-flight kicks in, and they choose to fight—even if they only harm themselves. They ignore Desmond Tutu's wise words, "Don't raise your voice, improve your argument."[40]

In such moments, the best thing to do is follow the advice of jiu jitsu fighters when they are caught in an inescapable hold: tap out. Further arguing only risks permanent loss. An investor might stop taking your calls and share with others that you refuse to accept no. That turns a bad, yet isolated, incident into a bad—and enduring—hit to your reputation.

Learning to Fall

There is an old saying often attributed to Buddha: "Pain is inevitable, but suffering is a choice." In martial arts, this is internalized in one of the first things you learn—how to fall. I have been taught that falling is inevitable, so you have to have a *break fall*, limiting the amount of damage you take. This doesn't prevent things from hurting, but it saves you from breaking bones.

In fundraising, break falls take many forms—some healthier and more productive than others. Some fundraisers respond to failure with humor, while others respond with anger or resentment. Some slip into denial, ignoring the event entirely, while others move on through acceptance.

To get over a tough loss, you might engage in meditation, rest, or exercise. I know some fundraisers who perk themselves up by looking at their bank account, comforted by the success they've already had and the certainty of the success they'll no doubt have in the future. It reminds them that these low moments are worth it and don't go on forever.

I know others who go out partying with their friends, affirming that they're still liked and popular. Fundraisers who prefer a quieter life may spend a peaceful evening with friends and family to bask in unconditional love and remind themselves why they're doing this.

Some fundraisers indulge in a hobby, losing themselves in a sport, craft, or outdoor activity, so they don't have to think about what happened. Others jump immediately into their next fundraising project. They want that sense of control, that feeling they can erase today's loss with tomorrow's big win.

Ultimately, a break fall is a personal choice. It's about finding what you need to do to reduce the harm that's been done to your ego so you can get back to the next pitch in the next room with the next investor.

For me, the most powerful break fall is the reliance on the Tao itself.

The more I believe authentically in the product, the more I am able to bring my best to every pitch. I believe these investments are going to change the world. When I hear that final no, I'm disappointed that I failed myself, my group, and my mission, but I know I've given my best.

There's comfort in knowing that things worked out how they should: I gave it an authentic try, and my product didn't fit the investor. I delivered the best possible pitch, using all the tools at my disposal that I have practiced for decades. If they still say no, that's what's supposed to happen. Two people met in the room, and one of them realized this wasn't right for them. If I was genuine and transparent and practiced my technique effectively, I can live with that.

I can also learn from it. I can refine my practice based on what took place in the room and improve my odds the next time I'm there. If the product was a good fit and I got the pitch wrong, I know this loss will serve to enrich my practice of the Tao. I can dive back in and get better where my technique failed me. If I'm going to change the world, I tell myself, I've got to capture the next one.

I can learn to deprioritize a certain persona or to emphasize a certain tactic to increase desire in the next meeting—because I believe in this product. I know this money should get raised—it needs to get raised—and if I improve, I can raise it the next time.

Chapter 12

Impactful Living

I initially developed the ideas in this book for one simple reason: I wanted to be successful in my work. My aim in researching and practicing these tools was to further my career. Back then, I wasn't a big name in the fundraising world. I was young and hungry and looking for a way to gain an advantage in my efforts to get the attention of investors. The value of these ideas, as far as I saw it back then, went no further.

It wasn't until I worked with the brilliant executive coach Jim Dethmer that I began to see the full value of the ideas I've presented in this book. When I joined one of his Conscious Learning Group forums, Dethmer revealed to me just how desperate I truly was for change. My exploration and training had lived up to its promise professionally and made me extremely successful in the fundraising space—but the thrill of that success was gone. Wins had begun to feel empty. Worst of all, I felt hollow. The person I presented in the room felt inauthentic. The work didn't reflect my truer self.

But how could I change this? Authentic living is highly prized and difficult to achieve. As I pondered this dilemma, the solution occurred to me: I already had all the tools I needed in my fundraising training. The same insights into persuasion and the same theory of mind could help me unlock a more authentic version of myself in every aspect of life.

As I applied these tools to myself, I found that they made me more empathetic and more aware of my own desires and fears. They helped me cultivate an authentic purpose. And in a surprise even to me, they made me far happier.

Incredibly, these benefits then flowed back into my work as a fundraiser. They influenced the projects I chose, infused my efforts with a new clarity of purpose, and changed the entire scope of my career. In fact, it is no exaggeration to say that I could only have scaled from raising millions of dollars to raising billions by allowing the Tao to guide not just my work but my life.

The Tao's Impact Across Life

It would be impossible to fully quantify how the Tao has enriched my life beyond my career. Some benefits, as with any practice, have been as subtle as they are profound. As they say, "What you learn *anywhere* is what you learn *everywhere*."

For instance, with enough introspection, a master of swordplay may discover benefits in how they approach a conversation, and a physicist may find patterns in the markets. The same is true of the Tao of Fundraising.

That said, I have endeavored here to break down some of the most apparent benefits I have noticed in my own life—and that I suspect would be shared by all who follow this path—across the personal, social, and technical spheres.

Personal Impact

Developmental psychologist Robert Kegan categorized the development of the human mind into five basic stages.[41] They are

- the *impulsive* mind,
- the *instrumental* mind,
- the *socialized* mind,
- the *self-authoring* mind, and
- the *interconnected* mind.

Our first stage is the *impulsive mind*. This is when we're at our youngest, as infants, living solely by our impulses.

As we grow into children and adolescents, we enter the second stage, the *instrumental mind*. Here, our focus is on our needs and wants. At this point, we're pure desire. Every relationship is transactional. It's about what we have to do to get what we want. Rules, for instance, are followed not because we consider them just or worthwhile but because we do not wish to face consequences. Following the rules generally gets us what we want; disobeying them risks what we want. So, we follow the rules.

Stage three, the *socialized mind*, is where most adults end their journey. At this stage, we define ourselves by our social networks—by the connections that make up our family, work, and community. These connections provide us with our ideas and beliefs. We no longer view people solely as a means to an end. Instead, we swing around and care deeply about how others are experiencing us. At this stage, we sublimate our wants and needs to our obligations to others. It's easy to see this change in new parents, who suddenly put most of their own interests and even health needs aside for their child.

Again, the bulk of adults stay in stage three, but some make it to stage four: the *self-authoring mind*. Those of us who reach this point are able to define ourselves separately from our connections. We can step outside expectations and define our own ideas and beliefs. We no longer allow society to define what we want, but we also avoid regressing to just focusing on our own personal desires. Instead, we ask ourselves what we want to bring into the world.

And then there's stage five. This is the point that few ever reach, the *interconnected mind*. Those of us who reach this peak come to see self as always changing. We don't define ourselves by a role or a relationship. We can recognize the complexity of life and hold multiple ideas in mind at once. We can get beyond our own perspective and find compromises and alternatives that others don't see.

To be clear, I am not saying that I have achieved some state of higher development. Like everyone else in the world, I am a work in progress. I have good days and bad days. And I am allergic to those who think, *I'm so enlightened that I don't have to be better than everyone else all the time.* Instead, this is meant to be aspirational, a path we continue to try to walk further down.

I share all this with you because I believe the Tao can be a useful tool in helping you achieve higher stages of development and in enabling you to maximize your impact in each stage. For instance, at the instrumental mind stage, the Tao can help you fulfill your wants and needs, but it can also teach you that there is more to life than your individual desires, thereby elevating you to a socialized mind. With a socialized mind, the Tao can enable you to achieve far more for the benefit of your community. If you are working to improve the lives of your family, the Tao can unlock new opportunities for this. If you wish to improve your city, the Tao can open doors to that possibility.

At the same time, the Tao empowers you to take on a more independent, individual perspective, leading into the self-authoring mind. Once you are in that stage, the Tao helps define your new beliefs and live up to them. It also draws you toward an interconnected mind.

You cannot practice the Tao without recognizing the thoughts of the other person in the room and seeing the value in them. It is, at its core, an interconnected practice—one built on finding alternative ways forward through the act of co-creation. It's about getting beyond the base urge to rush in and break things to get what you want. It calls on you to develop an independent perspective that harnesses the energy of everyone in the room in order to achieve results with mutual benefits.

This is not the only way the Tao can provide personal impact in our lives. It can also shape how we present ourselves to the world. In practicing persona play, for example, we can learn to bring our desires to the surface and choose the version of ourselves that best achieves those desires.

Social Impact

Along the way to developing and refining yourself, the Tao can also enable you to better understand your world and shape it productively. The Tao is, fundamentally, a social practice, built on the Copernican theory that whoever you are talking to is, at least for a moment, the center of your universe. For that reason, the elements that allow you to be successful in persuading people to invest will also help you become more successful socially.

This is because the key component of the Tao is empathy. As David Foster Wallace mentioned in his brilliant graduation speech at Kenyon College in 2005, "To be self-centered is the default setting. People who can adjust their natural default-setting are often described as being 'well-adjusted,' which I suggest to you is not an accidental term."[42]

The Tao calls on us to become well-adjusted, to focus on the experience of others. To be successful in its practice, we have to concentrate our energies on others and read their emotional desires and fears. What the other person in the room needs guides what we do next.

Armed with empathy, the tools of persuasion can provide us with profound value in our social interactions. As we've already seen, the same process used to sell cars can be the process to attract friends and make connections in your community.

At the same time, using the Karpman Drama Triangle, you can escape family arguments as easily as you remove the victims and villains in a conversation with an investor. And the same *logos*, *ethos*, and *pathos* motivations you speak to when raising a fund can persuade friends or a spouse to come to a mutually beneficial decision.

Just think about the last fight you had with a loved one. Was there a "villain" or a "victim" in the story? If it was a fight, then the answer is 100 percent *yes* because all fights are underpinned by someone believing they have the "right" to be angry at someone else. Simply recognizing that you are in this "drama loop" can help loosen your grip on the situation and recruit some of the other tools that the Tao teaches about changing someone's mind.

To overcome that framework next time, perhaps you could use Cialdini and build an argument from Authority or Consensus. Find someone or something that you both believe in and use that as a lens through which to explore the quality of the argument. Or be generous with seeing the other person's point in the hopes that they will be mature enough to reciprocate with a thoughtfulness of their own. Just as these tools work when implemented in the great drama of the investor's room, they also work on the smaller stages of life, whether you're discussing how to manage your family's spending or trying to talk your way out of a speeding ticket. If you want to convince your town council to build a new park or get a promotion for the crazy amount of money you just raised for your firm, the same techniques apply.

However, this doesn't give you the right to control someone. Your spouse can still veto your movie choice on date night, and your child can still be angry that you want them to do their homework. But you can better influence those decisions and, ideally, move into a world of co-creation in every relationship and every situation.

Intentional Training

The Tao is limitless, which means it would be impossible to include all its nuances within one book. Many concepts that have received only a brief mention deserve whole chapters. For instance, there is real value in physical fitness because the more attractive and stronger we appear to others, the more Authority they tend to grant us. Physical attractiveness makes it easier to persuade, and so we should make ourselves as attractive to others as possible—at least within reason.

I also recommend honing the art of enunciation. Before every important meeting or speech, I practice over-enunciating every word to help me speak with confidence and clarity when the real performance begins. Voice and acting coaches often make this a foundational exercise because of how powerfully it impacts their students' performances.

Additionally, there is great value in practicing meditation and heart rate variability (HRV) training to lower stress and improve mental clarity.[43] When I am working from home, I always have a heart monitor hooked up so I can observe how stress affects my heart rate. HRV allows me to be aware of how my body is physically reacting to different stress inputs so I can better control them. In the words of Tom Demarco, the pioneering software engineer and developer of structured analysis, "You can't control what you can't measure."[44]

This is really just the beginning. Again, the Tao is limitless. Almost any skill or insight can be added to it. The key, though, as in so much of life, is to integrate every tool through the combination of proper technique, intentional practice, and thorough preparation. Or, if you'll allow me to provide one last equation:

Talent + Training = Skill

Carol Dweck, in her groundbreaking book *Mindset*, talks about the "10,000-hour rule," by which someone can master any skill if they put in 10,000 hours of practice.[45] There has been some debate about the necessity of "natural talent" to achieve mastery. But necessary or not, even those without natural talent can become skilled with enough training and practice.

Ultimately, there's no magic here. Whether you wish to master a martial art or the art of persuasion, the same equation holds true. In every area of your life, from your efforts to be a better parent to your desire to improve your golf swing, sustainable success demands preparation, technique, and intentional effort while doing the reps. As Jim Rohn put it, "Success is nothing more than a few simple disciplines, practiced every day; while failure is simply a few errors in judgment, repeated every day."[46]

Preparation combines an element of practice with an element of planning. You plan around your strengths and weaknesses. Ask yourself:

- *What are my best qualities as a parent or a community member?*
- *Where am I weakest as a spouse or in casual conversation?*
- *What could go wrong, and how will I address it through my practice?*

With preparation and training, you can use your new mastery to find a path forward even when everything goes wrong. In such moments, you can be guided by Marcus Aurelius: "What stands in the way becomes the way."[47]

To see this technical impact in action, simply watch one of the classic matches of tennis legend Roger Federer. In the early sets, you can see the quality of his preparation. He has practiced every technique intentionally and studied the opponent. He knows how he intends to attack and defend, and he knows the likely strategy of the person on the opposite side of the net. But sometimes, in the fifth set, you'll see the plan isn't working. Rafael Nadal or Pete Sampras or Novak Djokovic has made adjustments. Federer is nursing a cramp or a slight muscle strain. He's tired, and his plan alone isn't going to be enough to get him over the line. In such moments, you can see his complete mastery ultimately take over. He has gone through the motions so many times, done so many volleys, lobs, and chips, he can rely on instinct. The most incredible shots seem to come out of nowhere. All because Federer has developed mastery over every aspect of his craft.

This same dynamic exists in fundraising and across all aspects of life. Whether we want to get better at persuading the other person in the room with us, become better parents, or develop our skill as an artist, natural talent is always helpful, but true mastery requires preparation, planning, and practice.

Authentic Living

When you allow the Tao to impact the personal, social, and technical sides of your life, an interesting thing happens. You begin to live more authentically. You can be more intentional in your behavior, acting the way you want to act with others. You can more clearly perceive what you want from life and a path to achieving it. While you can adjust your persona, you find you are more centered in who you are.

And if you nurture that authenticity, it will further improve your performance in the investment arena. Greater authenticity throughout your life allows for greater authenticity as a fundraiser. With a greater sense of self and greater control over the self, you can find greater motivation to sell and greater certainty in what you want to sell.

Additionally, expanding the Tao into your life allows you to find new techniques to add to your newly realized authentic practice. Again, the Tao is very flexible. It has no set limits. You may find that the voice lessons you take for the speeches you give in your community offer you better tone and control in the room. Techniques you discover to calm your children when throwing a fit may be adaptable for assuaging the upset investor.

This creates a natural virtuous cycle, as you find greater enrichment and a greater sense of self in life, and these realizations, in turn, create the opportunity to be a better fundraiser.

Chapter 13

Don't Lose Yourself

Some time ago, I was scammed out of a significant amount of money. I won't go into the details here. Instead, I want to focus on how it happened.

I met the CEO of an up-and-coming business. He had an incredible personal story and a magnetic personality. At every point where I would normally be skeptical, he seemed to have just the right answer. He fed my unspoken desires to help unlock resources for those who need them (e.g., my desire to be *heroic*). He quieted my usual skeptical fear by making me feel like a trusted adviser and close friend. He could seamlessly switch between the persona of a friendly, informal acquaintance eager to learn from my business knowledge and the persona of a bold, clear-sighted executive ready to march his company into a bright future.

Amazingly, he'd never trained in the Tao. He came by all these skills naturally and through a rather tortured upbringing that taught him some unique lessons about how to survive on his charm and create the illusion of Authority through lies and deceit. But make no mistake, he was a master. He was so brilliant at the art of persuasion that when his company went bankrupt, it seemed to come out of nowhere—not just for me but for many other canny investors. He'd had the whole world fooled.

I have been part of thousands of deals, raised billions of dollars, and worked with some of the most prominent business minds in the world. I've met with presidents. I've put together this first definitive book on the Tao of Fundraising. I mention this here only to show the power of these ideas. The same tactics I have cultivated and come to recognize around the world *worked on me.*

That is their power. And that is the danger when that power is abused.

The Dark Side of the Tao

The Tao is responsible for many of the great things in our lives. On a micro level, it is responsible for maintaining our individual strong connections and social bonds. On a macro level, it has allowed us to make business deals and raise funds for all the societal advances we enjoy. Every time someone discovers a cure for a disease that has been a scourge for generations, the Tao played a part. Every time a new technology comes out that makes our lives easier or more fun, the Tao was there.

The Tao of Fundraising in its most beautiful form is a means to take a product or idea you truly believe in and open the minds of people who might come to share that same enthusiasm. You redirect their logic, emotions, and values to come to a decision or preference that wasn't there before—ideally, for everyone's benefit.

This is the act of persuasion. In its most authentic form, persuasion inspires and enlightens people by introducing an idea to them in a way that allows you to get past their egoic defenses, all so you can guide them along the best possible course.

But these tools aren't always benevolent. We can see this in persuasion's dark twin: *manipulation*. Manipulation occurs when someone uses the same tools of persuasion we've covered in this book to convince others to do something solely for the benefit of the manipulator. They want you to buy a product not because it will make your life better but simply for their personal profit. And they'll do whatever it takes to convince you to do so. The scammers, the cheats, and the frauds of the world are all using the same techniques and achieving their aims by using—or *misusing*—the Tao.

We can see this tension at play in politics. Choose any issue. In climate change, there are legitimate disagreements, and persuasion is used by well-meaning actors to push for everything from an immediate transition to clean energy to a greater focus on developing carbon capture technology. Different people might champion government investment or removing regulations to encourage free market solutions.

All of those positions can come from an authentic place—but they often don't. Some choose not to debate the facts and adverse outcomes, instead resorting to crass manipulation. They know the facts of climate change, but they use the techniques of the Tao to convince others to ignore those facts. They manipulate people because it benefits them specifically, even at great harm to those they convince.

Likewise, many engage in persuasion for various perspectives on immigration—everything from open borders to increased high-skilled immigration to a focus on border security first and foremost. However, others demagogue, manipulating their listeners by blaming every social ill on immigrants or hand-waving away every legitimate concern about the country's immigration policy, even when they know their perspective doesn't match reality.

Persuasion and manipulation are opposite sides of the same coin, and the side it lands on for each practitioner of the Tao depends on their ego. As we know by now, the *ego* is the part of human consciousness entirely focused on its own desires. The Tao's tools are designed to navigate through egoic structures. Whether it is *logos*, *ethos*, *pathos*, fear, or the Drama Triangle, the Tao shows us a path around the ego's defenses to get to a mutually beneficial solution.

You can navigate all the egos in the room with authenticity and integrity. In chapter 11, I spoke about the importance of ego deprivation. Through the Tao, we reduce our focus on our own ego and instead focus on the desires and fears of the other person in the room. We sublimate our own ego to put another first. In this way, we practice the Tao on ourselves as we practice on others. We're using them, in a sense, to decrease our own fear, understand our own desires, and become aware of our own drama and personas, all so we can *move beyond* ego to co-creation.

But what if you recognized the desires and fears of the other person in the room while refusing to sublimate your own ego? Instead of ego deprivation, the Tao becomes a tool of ego reinforcement. In that case, all that matters is getting *you* what *you* want. You aim to completely satisfy your ego. Your ego has to win. Your ego refuses to accept no. Your ego demands fulfillment using any means necessary.

You are no longer interested in a mutually beneficial solution. Any solution must give you everything you want. The effects on the other in the room are at most incidental.

Protecting Yourself Against the Dark Side

I want to end this book with something of a warning. The Tao is a dangerous thing to learn. Like a martial art, it can hurt other people. An experienced martial artist never throws the first punch. The samurai doesn't draw their sword first. A master of such techniques is far too aware of the destruction that can result from abusing their skills.

Likewise, the tools for successful fundraising are the same tools that allow a person to gaslight their spouse, abuse the trust of their friends, and commit fraud on a Bernie Madoff scale. It is possible to take everything you've learned in this book and convince your friends to give you all of their savings. You can affect the right persona to earn trust in whatever vision you're selling. You can hit them on their *ethos*, showing how giving you money is the right thing to do. You can play on their *pathos* by reminding them of every time you were there for them. You can develop a strong *logos* by showing them how giving you money just makes sense. You can eliminate every fear and put your-self in the role of their personal hero who can solve all the drama in their lives. You can move through the entire sales cycle and use the Laws of Fundraising to make sure you take a big enough bite from each member of your friend group to achieve whatever you want.

And if you are a master of all these techniques, it will work. It's worked over and over again throughout history. It's worked on me. It's worked on every victim in every Ponzi scheme. It's worked on wise and diligent investors across every era. And the perpetrators are not always mustache-twisting villains, either. Often, they are people like you and me—at least at first. They start out ethical. But then they encounter some bad luck. They land in a hole. They've misjudged an investment or overspent. The consequences of doing the right thing seem too severe. So, they dabble in the Tao's magic to get a little breathing room. Then they go a little further, doubling down. Once they've gotten too deep in the hole, they find the only way to sustain their success is to keep breaking their ethical rules.

I am not trying to point fingers on this. I know that none of us are completely immune to the dark side of the Tao because I know that I have crossed my own professional eth-ical lines in the past. I have convinced people to invest when I didn't believe it was a profitable investment. I did it for my own personal gain. I didn't break any laws, and I didn't do immense harm. But I still feel I am lesser for those experiences.

Unfortunately, many practitioners of the Tao's tech-niques have felt no compulsion to pull back and return to the light. Just look around our society, and you'll see that such behavior has caused us all great harm.

So, my parting message in this book is to put you on guard against slipping to the dark side of the Tao yourself. The first way to protect yourself is to be aware of—and beware of—the easy first steps in the wrong direction.

Creating Unfair Advantages

Throughout this book, I have touched briefly on the darker ways to leverage the Tao.

It's undeniable, for instance, that when people dress well and are in shape, it's easier for them to persuade others. But there's a reason I only mentioned this advantage briefly. It's very easy to take that advice and push it beyond the ethical. Sexuality is a powerful persuasion device, as we all know. Of course, it's possible to use sexuality in a way that strengthens all the other techniques in this book. However, such tactics fall at the very least in an ethical gray area. In essence, using sex appeal isn't about redirecting around the ego to allow space for persuasion; it's about distracting the ego enough that the person in the room agrees to anything.

This isn't the only kind of unfair advantage you can introduce into the Tao. Tools like guilt and bullying also fall outside of a more authentic and ethical practice. Imagine the power of a *pathos* argument when boosted with a huge helping of guilt. Consider how effective the use of *ethos* is when there's a hint of a threat to publicize the other person's actions. These tactics reduce the space for someone to make a genuine decision, forcing their hand.

The same is true when deliberately eschewing transparency. If you know a product has major issues yet to be resolved but hide that information, you aren't allowing the other person in the room to make an informed, honest decision. You may get what you want in that case, but you've failed as a partner in co-creation.

The Light Side

The only way to avoid moving to the dark side of the Tao is to commit to the light. Mindfulness, integrity checks, and surrounding yourself with people who can hold you accountable are all important defenses against this slide. Use break falls to learn from failure instead of nursing grudges. Set lines and don't cross them. Decide now where *too far* is and refuse to enter that unethical space.

Place a premium on your reputation and remind yourself how quickly you can lose it once you turn to the dark side.

These are all valuable ways to protect yourself, but there are further steps you can take to ensure that you practice the Tao for the right reasons.

Expose the Tricks

Unfortunately, there's no way to guarantee the Tao won't be practiced on you. I'm a living example of that. However, you can usually spot these practices in action. Just as a professional magician can work out how other performers achieve their illusions most of the time, a master of the Tao will pick up on even quite artful efforts at manipulative persuasion.

That provides you with some protection, and it also puts you in a position to protect others. In this way, the Tao is as much a defensive art as it is an offensive one.

I once advised a colleague on whether to take a position at a new company. This colleague recounted her most recent conversation with the CEO, who was trying to recruit her. The CEO conceded that he wasn't going to pay her what she was worth, but he tried to manipulate her by tugging at her *ethos*.

"I know how much you believe in this company's mission," he had told her.

From my perspective, that was a dirty trick. The company could afford to pay her better. They were trying to save money by abusing the Tao. So, I over-indexed on her *ethos* to counter the CEO.

"If that's what really matters to you," I said, "you could go raise money for orphans. If these people want you to work for them, their mission isn't enough to justify their offer."

In an instant, that CEO's argument that had almost persuaded my friend was exposed for what it was. Recognizing that put her in a position to negotiate fair compensation.

Once you know the tools of the Tao, you will see them everywhere. They're in our conversations. They're in our advertising. They're in our political speeches. And recognizing the tricks as they're played can allow you to call them out and remove much of their power.

This was actually the perspective that Robert Cialdini brought to his own work, whose tools of persuasion we covered in chapter 7. He wrote *Influence* not as a text for advertisers and salespeople but in large part as a defensive tool *against* those forces. The aim was to educate people on how they were being manipulated.

I recommend bringing this same spirit to your own practice. While this book has been "offensive" in its focus—because the aim is to persuade investors—it should be equally employed defensively against those who abuse these ideas.

Embrace Guilt

I know countless people on Wall Street who are miserable in their jobs. They keep coming into the office every day because they use some forms of *logos, ethos,* and *pathos* to rationalize away their dystopia. They remind themselves of their desires to maintain a lifestyle stocked with big houses and boats, and they find logical, ethical, and emotional reasons why those desires should trump their misery at work.

Sometimes, the best way to break free of the hold the darker side of the Tao has on you is by allowing yourself to feel the emotion lurking underneath: *guilt*. Guilt can be negative when it is overrepresented in your emotional makeup, but it serves a natural, valuable purpose. Its presence suggests that you have broken your own code in some fashion. It's a crack in your egoic wall. It's a warning that something you're doing is wrong.

Importantly, this is the nature of guilt but not of *shame*. According to social worker and author Brené Brown, shame lacks such value because it connects to a more holistic sense of self.[48] Shame is something *you think you are*. It convinces you that something is inherently bad about you, and it affects your self-worth. But if that quality exists within your very nature, you can excuse yourself for any moral failing. If you cheat on your partner, you can dismiss your behavior as inevitable. You're just a cheater by nature. The act represents a failure of the soul.

Guilt, on the other hand, recognizes your culpability. Your transgression was not inevitable and not tied to some inescapable flaw in your emotional, mental, and physical makeup; rather, guilt spotlights the fact that you *decided* to cheat. It's a sign you failed your true self.

It is tempting when experiencing guilt to turn the Tao on that guilt and use those tools to cover up the crack in your moral foundation. Do not do this. Instead, use guilt as a barometer—as a means to see where you are deceiving yourself. Then, when those problem areas are revealed, you can use the Tao to repair the damage to your inner self and your relationships.

Further the Causes of Light

The best way to remain on the right course with the Tao is to focus on using these tools for the right reasons. You may not be in a position to start raising funds for charities or other noble causes immediately, but wherever possible, your aim should be to ensure that money goes where it can do the most good and help the most people.

You can also utilize the tools of persuasion to promote active, positive change in your life and at work. You can advocate to increase benefits for those who are often left outside of the room. You can push for more diversity in those rooms. You can seek to level the playing field and create a fairer system.

Whatever causes you feel most passionate about—whether it's workers' rights, the environment, or the state of our politics—apply the Tao to help achieve better outcomes. These are powerful tools. Make sure you use them for noble purposes.

Live by Your Code

As we discussed in chapter 1, in feudal Japan there was a type of warrior called a rōnin. These were wandering samurai with no lord or master over them.

In the films of Akira Kurasawa, the rōnin comes to play an interesting ethical role. They are the masters of violence, and they are largely unrestrained by local laws. But they honor the samurai code of *bushido*. For this very reason, they also become the masters of the ethical. In films like *Yojimbo* and *Seven Samurai*, they are heroes, standing up for the common good against those who would abuse others for their own betterment.

It is, admittedly, perhaps idealistic to aim for a world in which those who follow the Tao also seek a similar path, but it is my great hope. The Tao, like the rōnin, contains violence and a code of ethics to restrain that violence. It is possible to have one without the other, but such a world is not one we want to live in.

That is the world of *Yojimbo*, which means *bodyguard* in Japanese.[49] In that film, the rōnin, played by the great Toshiro Mifune, enters a village caught up in a war between two groups, each led by a different type of master of violence: the mercenary. These mercenaries work for the highest bidder and will perform any act without any ethical qualm. They will intimidate, pillage, and murder if it advances their singular interest in profit and power.

They fear only two things: missing out on any financial gain and those powerful enough to take their current gains away.

Perhaps you know of such mercenaries in the financial world today.

The only consistent good in the world of *Yojimbo* is the rōnin, who seeks always to protect the weak and harms only those who would harm others. In this world, he is happy to make money from his services—there's no conflict in acting as a bodyguard for one warlord or another—but only when it does no unethical harm to others. And while it is never spelled out directly, it is this decency and moral good that gives him that extra strength, that edge that allows him to defeat the mercenaries and save the village.

While I encourage you to use the tools we have covered in this book to advance your career and make your fortune in the world, I also hope you will take what you have learned further and use it for the good of all. I hope you will choose the path of the rōnin over the mercenary: to defend others against the abuse of these ideas and to persuade people to follow a better course where possible.

That is the ultimate potential of the Tao, and it is now in your hands.

CONCLUSION

Recently, I made a huge decision. Months ago, a company I founded with some friends, Lila Sciences, achieved some significant breakthroughs that led to a very successful fundraising outcome for the company. Lila's aim is to transform how humanity will do science. If Lila succeeds in its ambitions, it will supercharge the rate of human discovery and unlock currently unimaginable breakthroughs.

This was simply too big an opportunity to watch from the sidelines. So, my partners and I decided that I should take on the twin roles of chairman of the board and president of corporate development. This role will include some fundraising—we just raised an astonishing $550 million on our Series A funding, thanks to the Tao and my efforts—but I will be concentrating primarily on new responsibilities.

In real time, then, this book has transformed from a playbook by a seasoned fundraiser to my farewell to the profession.

As I've mulled over this radical change in my career, I've come to realize that this book is a "love letter" to the industry that has accompanied me on so much of my journey. Fundraising has helped me grow into the person I am today. Without fundraising, I never could have taken on this role at Lila because I never would have discovered the Tao.

Even before this opportunity, the Tao had already allowed me to take part in so much that is good in the world. In particular, it has allowed me to jump into the middle of other people's worlds and learn about their perspective, psychology, and beliefs.

Many years ago, one my children asked me, "Dad, what do you think your purpose in life is?" Without hesitating, I said, "Well, my purpose is to provide resources to good people so they can do great things."

This answer, of course, was idealistic—which I think is inherent to the nature of purpose—and it wasn't always true of my work. In the beginning, I found myself fundraising for people whose character or mission weren't completely aligned with my values. To escape this predicament, I improved my skills using the Tao to the point that I could choose the people I worked for. It was the Tao, in other words, that allowed me to turn my talents toward those good people and their great causes.

The Tao has been responsible for the two greatest rewards from my work—setting aside financial gains, which have been an obvious and profound blessing in their own way. But the rewards I have in mind have brought me a deeper and more profound joy.

The first significant benefit that I will take away from this vocation is the relationships I've made. This job has allowed me to grow close to some of the most driven and interesting people in the world. No matter their station in life, most people need more resources than they currently have in order to fulfill their ambitions. Throughout my journey, my skills as a fundraiser have given me access to people who are trying to make a difference in this world. Many of them have become very good friends, and all of them have been a gift to my life, as I hope I've been a gift to theirs.

The other benefit affects how I see the nature of truth. In many ways, this insight is almost spiritual. Through fundraising, I've discovered that the world does have some universal truths—the "it is what it is" facts of life—but the majority of our existence is spent constructing our sense of reality from those things that fall short of undebatable truth. We cobble together this sense of reality through our experiences and beliefs, and this creates a personal sense of truth. Realizing this fact led me to the habit of seeing what is right about what the other person in the room is saying.

This revelation may sound simple—even obvious—but to fully absorb it requires a profound rewiring of perception. Humans have evolved to focus our attention on what is wrong with the world. Scientists call this the negativity bias, and it's served us well throughout our history—because this negativity bias also motivates us to try to fix things. Thanks to our negativity bias, we've learned to avoid dangerous situations and to develop solutions that make our lives safer and more comfortable.

For the most part, we still train ourselves to utilize this bias in our favor. MBA degrees, coaching, and management training all focus on helping business leaders discover what is wrong and think critically about how to fix it. We are taught to focus our minds on finding the inefficiencies or deficiencies, and we develop a whole toolbox of potential solutions to address them—all so we can move on to the next problem.

Through the Tao, I came to realize that the secret of fundraising is to reverse this wiring. All the tools and all the frameworks in this book grow out of one question: *What is the other person saying that is right?*

How do they believe the world should work? What are the solutions they believe can fix it? What can I do to help them make the world reflect that perspective?

In a way, this is the root intuition that evolved into my Copernican theory of fundraising. Place the other person's experience first. See the world through their eyes. And find out what is right about that view.

Once I understood this, I became far more persuasive. When I could change my story to represent their worldview, I found I had a more eager and interested audience. If I recognized they were stuck in the Karpman Drama Triangle, I found I could end up on their side—even when I started as the villain. When I approached Cialdini from a desire to help persuade them of what I thought was in their best interest, I was able to apply it far more successfully. This perspective has transformed my life far beyond my career. It has trained a certain humility into me—a humility that has developed into a kind of serenity.

When I'm at my best professionally, personally, romantically, or spiritually, I'm looking for what is right about everything that is going on. I'm looking to see what others believe is right so I can do my part to make the world match their best vision of it.

I will take this perspective with me to Lila Sciences—because, as the Tao teaches, fundraising never ends. The wisdom to see what is good in this world will be with me everywhere I go.

This is my final lesson for you in this book. With this one insight, you can undoubtedly become a more successful fundraiser. But it has more to offer than that. When you truly begin to see what is right about the world, you'll find you aren't just fundraising; you're making the world a better place, one sales call at a time.

ACKNOWLEDGMENTS

This book is a summation of my career as a fundraiser, and so, in a sense, it is the result of decades of research, experimentation, and contemplation. Over those many years, there have been hundreds of people who have contributed in larger and smaller ways to the ideas within these pages. It would be impossible to thank them all.

So, I will limit myself to a few names that have made the biggest impact on my career and my thinking. I'll start with all the sales mentors who showed me that persuasion is less about changing minds than it is about illuminating what was already true. Jerry Della Femina, David Fialkow, Scott Jenson, Sean O'Brien, John Pasnau, and Steve Volkers: the Tao would not exist without you.

And to all the people who helped bring this book to life—in particular, Mike Bolner, Jim Dethmer, Chris Fussell, Mary Perea, Tim Peek, and Josh Waitzkin— thank you for lending me your minds, your patience, and your faith.

Finally, I want the last words I write in this book to be to my family. Jodi, Annabel, Charlie, and Maggie: the Tao has led me on a wonderful journey, but I'm grateful that every path always leads back to you.

NOTES

Introduction

1. Victor H. Mair, preface to *Tao Te Ching*, by Lao Tsu (Bantam Books, 1990).
2. Graham Duncan, "The Playing Field," *GrahamDuncan .com* (blog), accessed July 25, 2025, https://grahamduncan .blog/the-playing-field/.

Chapter 1

3. Karl Alexander, Doris Entwisle, Linda Olson, *The Long Shadow: Family Background, Disadvantaged Urban Youth, and the Transition to Adulthood* (Russell Sage Foundation, 2014).
4. David Jagielki, "If You Invested $10,000 in Moderna at the End of 2019, This Is How Much You Would Have Today," *The Motley Fool* (blog), accessed August 6, 2025, https:// www.fool.com/investing/2024/01/21/if-you-invested-10000 -in-moderna-in-2019/.
5. Sun Tzu, *The Art of War*, trans. Lionel Giles (Barnes & Noble Books, 2000), pg. 5.

6. Exodus 13:17: "When Pharaoh let the people go, God did not lead them on the road through the Philistine country, though that was shorter. For God said, 'If they face war, they might change their minds and return to Egypt.' (NIV).

Chapter 2

7. Malcolm Gladwell, *David and Goliath: Underdogs, Misfits, and the Art of Battling Giants* (Back Bay Books, 2015).
8. 1 Samuel 17:33 NIV.
9. Sun Tzu, *The Art of War*, trans. Lionel Giles. 1.24
10. Shane Parrish, host, *The Knowledge Project*, podcast, "Leading Above the Line," June 18, 2019, https://podcasts.apple.com/us/podcast/60-jim-dethmer-leading-above-the-line/id990149481?i=1000441920107.

Chapter 3

11. Alan Taylor, dir., "Smoke Gets in Your Eyes," *Mad Men*, season 1, episode 1, aired July 19, 2007, on AMC.

Chapter 5

12. "O.J. Simpson Defense: 'If It Doesn't Fit, You Must Acquit,'" posted June 9, 2014, by CNN, YouTube, 2:07, https://www.youtube.com/watch?v=NH-VuP_5cA4.

Chapter 6

13. William Shakespeare, *Julius Caesar*, 3.2.21-26.
14. Shakespeare, *Julius Caesar*, 3.2.82-89.
15. Shakespeare, *Julius Caesar*, 3.2.116-17.

16. "Climbing Mount Everest Is Work For Supermen; A Member of Former Expeditions Tells of the Difficulties Involved in Reaching the Top—Hope of Winning in 1924 by Establishment of Base Camps on a Higher Level," *New York Times*, March 18, 1923, https://www.nytimes.com /1923/03/18/archives/climbing-mount-everest-is-work-for -supermen-a-member-of-former.html.

17. Will Kenton, "Self-Interest: What It Means in Economics, with Examples," *Investopedia* (blog), June 7, 2025, https:// www.investopedia.com/terms/s/self-interest.asp.

Chapter 7

18. Citation for Chris Fussell's story? E.g., A conversation with the author, date, place . . .

19. Robert Cialdini, *Influence: The Psychology of Persuasion* (Harper Business, 2021).

20. Cialdini, *Influence*.

21. See Robert Frost, "The Road Not Taken," Poetry Foundation, https://www.poetryfoundation.org/poems/44272/the -road-not-taken.

22. "The End," written by Paul McCartney, track 16 on the Beatles, *Abbey Road*, Apple Records, 1969.

23. George Grow, "Monkeys Cooperate and Share," Voice of America, May 17, 2000, https://www.manythings.org/voa /animals/6002.html.

24. Francis Ford Coppola, dir., *The Godfather*, Paramount Pictures, 1972.

25. Joel Roberts, "Kerry's Top Ten Flip-Flops," CBS News, September 29, 2004, https://www.cbsnews.com/news/kerrys -top-ten-flip-flips/.

26. Roberts, "Kerry's Top Ten Flip-Flops."

27. Vindu Goel, "Yahoo's Brain Drain Shows a Loss of Faith Inside the Company," *New York Times*, January 10, 2016, https://www.nytimes.com/2016/01/11/technology/yahoos -brain-drain-shows-a-loss-of-faith-inside-the-company.html.

Chapter 8

28. Stephen B. Karpman, "Fairy Tales and Script Drama Analysis," *Transactional Analysis Bulletin* 7, no. 26 (1968): 39–43, https://calisphere.org/item/52ceb48d-c76a-4df3-934d -88d7096f3b29/.

29. Jim Dethmer, *The 15 Commitments of Conscious Leadership* (Dethmer, Chapman, and Klemp, 2015).

30. Plutarch, *The Life of Lucullus*, trans. Bernadotte Perrin (Loeb Classical Library, 1923).

31. Herodotus, *Histories*, trans. A. D. Godley (Loeb Classical Library, 1925).

32. William Shakespeare, *Antony and Cleopatra*, 2.5.78-79.

Chapter 9

33. Gay Hendricks, "To Have a Great Time All the Time, Play with Your Personas," Hendricks Institute, accessed September 26, 2025, https://hendricks.com/to-have-a-great-time -all-the-time-play-with-your-personas/?v=0b3b97fa6688.

34. Steven Zaillian, dir., *Searching for Bobby Fischer*, Paramount Pictures, 1993.

35. Will Storr, *The Status Game: On Social Position and How We Use It* (William Collins, 2021).

36. Scott Hornbacher, dir., "Dark Shadows," *Mad Men*, Season 5, Episode 9, aired May 13, 2012, on AMC.

Chapter 10

37. Benjamin VanHoose, "Chris Hemsworth Reveals Brother Liam Was 'Almost' Cast as Thor Instead: 'My Audition Sucked,'" *People*, July 8, 2022, https://people.com/movies/chris-hemsworth-brother-liam-hemsworth-was-almost-cast-as-thor-instead-of-him/.

38. Allegra Tepper, "Kerry Washington, Jake Gyllenhaal Honor Casting Directors at Artios Awards," *Variety*, November 19, 2013, https://variety.com/2013/scene/awards/kerry-washington-jake-gyllenhaal-honor-casting-directors-at-artios-awards-1200855539/.

39. Felix Richter, "Global Mask Sales Surged 30-Fold During the Pandemic, Statista, January 12, 2023, https://www.statista.com/chart/29100/global-face-mask-sales/.

Chapter 11

40. Desmond Tutu, "The Second Nelson Mandela Annual Lecture Address," lecture, Johannesburg, South Africa, November 23, 2004, https://www.nelsonmandela.org/news/entry/the-second-nelson-mandela-annual-lecture-address.

Chapter 12

41. Robert Kegan, *The Evolving Self: Problem and Process in Human Development* (Harvard University Press, 1982).

42. David Foster Wallace, "2005 Kenyon College Commencement Address," speech, Gambier, Ohio, May 21, 2005.

43. "Heart Rate Variability: How It Might Indicate Well-Being," Harvard Health Publishing, April 3, 2024, https://www.health.harvard.edu/blog/heart-rate-variability-new-way-track-well-201711212789.

44. Tom Demarco, *Controlling Software Projects: Management, Measurement and Estimation* (Yourdon Press, 1982), pg. 3.

45. Carol S. Dweck, *Mindset: The New Psychology of Success* (Ballantine Books, 2007).

46. Jim Rohn, *The Treasury of Quotes* (Success Books, 2006), pg. 26.

47. Marcus Aurelius, *Meditations*, 5.20.

48. Brené Brown, "Listening to Shame," posted March 1, 2012, by TED Talk, YouTube, https://www.youtube.com/watch?v=psN1DORYYV0.

49. Akira Kurasawa, dir., *Yojimbo*, Toho Co., 1961.

ABOUT THE AUTHOR

John Kim is one of the world's top fundraisers. He is currently the chairman and president of corporate development at Lila Sciences, a technology company combining advanced AI with real-world laboratory automation to dramatically accelerate scientific discoveries. He was previously the chief client officer at General Catalyst, a leading venture capital firm. He has also worked for investment firms such as J.P. Morgan, Court Square Capital, and Kelso & Company.

John graduated from Brown University magna cum laude with a degree in economics and began his career as a marketing representative at IBM.

John lives in Brooklyn with his wife and his three children. In his free time, he likes to spend time out on the water, strum his guitar and start a singalong with friends, practice jiu jitsu and enjoy a good slice of pizza (New York style, of course).

Seth Libby is a professional ghostwriter. He has written or edited more than fifty published books over the past decade.

He is the co-author of *Byline: How Local Journalists Can Improve the Global News Industry and Change the World.*

He lives in Bloomington, Indiana with his wife and two children.